The Evening Crowd at Kirmser's

The Evening Crowd at Kirmser's

A GAY LIFE IN THE 1940S

Ricardo J. Brown

Edited by William Reichard
Foreword by Allan H. Spear

University of Minnesota Press
Minneapolis — London

These stories are true. Only the names have been changed to protect the innocent.

Published by the University of Minnesota Press
111 Third Avenue South, Suite 290
Minneapolis, MN 55401-2520
http://www.upress.umn.edu

Library of Congress Cataloging-in-Publication Data

Brown, Ricardo J.
　　The evening crowd at Kirmser's : A gay life in the 1940s /
　Ricardo J. Brown ; edited by William Reichard ; foreword by
　Allan H. Spear.
　　　p.　cm.
　　ISBN 0-8166-3621-4 (alk. paper)
　　1. Homosexuality—Minnesota—Saint Paul—History. 2. Gays—
　Minnesota—Saint Paul—History.　I. Title.
　　HQ76.3.U52 S253 2001
　　306.76'6'09776581—dc21

2001000390

Printed in the United States of America on acid-free paper

The University of Minnesota is an equal-opportunity educator and employer.

11　10　09　08　07　06　05　04　03　02　01　　　10　9　8　7　6　5　4　3　2　1

One of the pleasures of writing a book is the opportunity to dedicate it. For Larry, who has the heart enough for both of us; for Lloyd, who still believes in Kansas; and for my sister, Elizabeth. Sisters are among the most remarkable of women.

Contents

Foreword

Allan H. Spear

*T*HE SECOND WORLD WAR was a watershed in gay and lesbian history in the United States. Thousands of gay men and a smaller, but significant, number of lesbians served in the military, and countless others left their homes to work in war plants and other civilian services related to the war effort. This mass mobilization, according to Allan Bérubé, whose *Coming Out Under Fire* first documented the gay and lesbian war experience, "propelled gay men and lesbians into the mainstream of American life" (299). Young men and women were torn away from constricted lives on farms and in small towns, separated from families, and exposed to the more cosmopolitan milieu of big cities, where most crucially, they found each other. In port cities and on military bases, on troopships and in actual combat, many gay people first came to realize that they were not alone in their sexual orientation and first became conscious of themselves as members of a minority within American society.

Gay people in Western society had long suffered from a special kind of oppression. Unlike members of racial or ethnic minorities, most gay men and lesbians were able to hide their identity. So long as their sexual orientation was secret, they could participate fully in all aspects of society. We now know of many closeted gay people who held high positions in government, religious life, business, and the arts. But closetry exacted a high price. Gay men and lesbians were forced to deny an important facet of their very being—their sexuality. They spun elaborate webs of lies and subterfuges to hide their sexual orientation from family, friends, and coworkers. Above all, they lived in constant fear of exposure. A casual slip, the slightest crack in the facade could lead to loss of job, loss of social status, rejection by family and friends, even criminal prosecution and jail. Gay people on both sides of the Atlantic drew cautionary lessons from the famous case of Oscar Wilde, whose 1895 trial for homosexual behavior brought him from the pinnacle of fame and fortune to humiliation, imprisonment, and ruin.

World War II did not end all of this. In fact, as Bérubé points out, the military formalized its screening process for homosexuality and rejected those it could identify as gay. Those who were inducted were frequently the victims of witchhunts and purges designed to drive "perverts" out of the military. Women in particular, who were volunteers and not draftees, were subject to continual surveillance by officials who feared that the women's branches would be viewed by the public as havens for lesbians. A gay man or lesbian discharged from the military for homosexuality customarily received an undesirable discharge—a stigma that carried over into civilian life.

Yet recent historical research reveals another side to gay and lesbian life in the first half of the twentieth century. Despite the fears and traumas of life in the closet, gay people began to forge communities. In our largest cities, these were communities of remarkable complexity. George Chauncey, in his path-breaking study, *Gay New York,* reconstructs a world of saloons and baths, of restaurants and rooming houses, where gay men met for sexual and social liaisons. In this exclusively gay world, men could drop the masks they were forced to wear at work or with family and fulfill needs that elsewhere went unmet. Chauncey's work interestingly parallels what happened in African American historiography in the 1960s and 1970s. African American historians, having documented the oppressive nature of slavery and Jim Crow, began to look at African American communities to see how in the face of oppression a people could adapt and survive and create a vigorous and vital culture. The trick in all of this is to maintain balance, to recognize the remarkable achievement of survival without minimizing the severity of the oppression.

World War II sharpened this tension between oppression and survival for gay men and women. The growing influence of psychiatry led to a gradual shift in thinking about homosexuality; rather than immoral sinners, gay men and women were now more likely to be viewed as psychological misfits. Yet this shift did little to lessen the marginality and furtiveness of gay life. The war expanded horizons. It allowed the kind of gay communities that Chauncey found in New York in the early twentieth century to take root and develop in smaller cities. But it did not lead to a frontal assault on society's assumptions about homosexuality, whether they were based on religion or psychiatry. As Bérubé notes, the generation of World War II veterans responded to a hostile environment "not [with] collective protest or political action . . . [but] by expanding their 'closet,' making it a roomier place to live." This was a crucial moment of transition. Earlier generations "had invented the closet," the system that enabled them to hide their homosexuality from a hostile world. A later generation would come out of the closet and live as openly gay men and women. "But the World War II generation slowly stretched their closet to its limits, not proclaiming or parading their homosexuality in public but not willing to live lonely, isolated lives" (Bérubé, 271).

The Evening Crowd at Kirmser's is a remarkable document of this transitional moment in gay and lesbian history. Set in 1945–46, it is the memoir of a World War II veteran, discharged from the navy for homosexuality, who returns to his hometown of St. Paul, Minnesota, and settles into life in this "expanded

closet." It centers on the habitués of a gay bar in downtown St.
Paul. Bérubé remarks that gay bars "evolved into the primary
gay social institutions in cities after the war" (271). Previously
limited to the largest cities, by the late 1940s gay bars were
opening in medium-size cities. "By providing patrons with
public spaces in which to gather, bars helped shape a sense
of gay identity that went beyond the individual to the group"
(27). This is precisely what happened in Kirmser's, the bar on
Wabasha Street that Ricardo Brown so vividly brings to life. A
seedy "dive," owned by a German immigrant couple struggling
to make ends meet, Kirmser's is taken over (in the evenings at
least) by gay men and lesbians for whom it becomes a second
home, a place where they can be themselves, drop their masks,
and develop relationships free of the lies and subterfuges that
otherwise dominate their lives.

The Evening Crowd at Kirmser's describes both the joys and
the traumas of gay life in the aftermath of the war. The men
and women who hang out at Kirmser's become a kind of surro-
gate family. They share secrets they cannot share with their real
families. They come to care about each other and develop a
sense of collective identity that provides a defense against the
insults and outrages hurled at them by a homophobic society.
But Brown never romanticizes Kirmser's. He is unflinching in
his description of the difficulties faced by gay people in the era
before Stonewall. Brown's own discharge from the navy is a
source of continual shame and anxiety; when he confesses to
high school friends, they are uncomfortable and try to hide
from him. His family could never know: "There was no greater
horror than having our own families shut us out." Unless it
was losing a job. It took only an anonymous note for Dale to
lose a job he had had for six years. "A job was a sacred thing,
something that all of us who were brought up in the depression knew was hard to come by." Despite their best efforts, gay
people could not always keep the closet door closed. When it
cracked open, ever so slightly, the results could be devastating.

"You could never let your guard down. You always had to watch for the signals and the traps."

Red Larson's fate summed up all of the fears of pre-Stonewall gay men. Here the Oscar Wilde tragedy came home to St. Paul. Caught having sex with another man in the backseat of an automobile, Larson was arrested, saw his name published in the newspaper, lost his job, and went to the workhouse. Worst of all, after his release, he was forbidden to associate with "known perverts," cutting him off from the only community he could call his own. He was left like a dead man: "Someone should have had the decency to close [his] eyes." Red Larson's friends could do nothing except thank God that they were not the ones who were caught.

Donald Webster Cory, the pseudonymous author of *The Homosexual in America* (1951), one of the earliest accounts of gay life written from a gay perspective, wrote that the "worst effect of discrimination has been to make the homosexuals doubt themselves and share in the general contempt for sexual inverts" (39). This "internalized homophobia," as it would be called today, is also apparent among the habitués of Kirmser's. While the bar, on the one hand, provided a refuge where "we could sit down among friends, people like us, and be ourselves," it did not give its patrons the strength or solidarity to stand up against the outside world. Brown is often snubbed when he runs into his Kirmser friends in other settings—especially if they are with family or coworkers. And in perhaps the most chilling episode in *The Evening Crowd at Kirmser's,* when Kirmser's itself is invaded and "Flaming Youth" is attacked by a couple of gay-bashing thugs, no one but Brown comes to his aid. In fact, Brown is the one whose conduct is questioned: "Why did you get into it?" Calling the police was out of the question: "We were the criminals." Becoming involved risked exposure. There was nothing to do but accept the victimization that was the lot of gay men and women.

Another vividly described incident further illustrates the

limitations of the brotherhood forged at Kirmser's. When Brown learns that Dickie Grant, a luckless, improvident, but essentially harmless member of the Kirmser's set, is sent to prison for writing bad checks and then murdered by a fellow inmate, he is outraged. "What kind of sadistic son of a bitch would send that harmless, girlish soul to a state penitentiary? . . . Dear God, you might as well pull the wings off a butterfly." And yet when he tries to express his rage to another friend from Kirmser's, the reaction is "Another fairy bites the dust." The larger society's trivialization of gay life had been accepted by gay people themselves.

The Evening Crowd at Kirmser's is primarily about being gay at a crucial moment in gay history. But it illuminates other themes as well. It is also about class. Chauncey's study of New York makes clear that class is an important factor in determining how gay people adapt to their status in society. Middle- and upper-class men had more space to expand their closets. In New York, by the 1920s, they had their own apartments, clubs, and social networks. Ricardo Brown and his friends, on the other hand, were distinctly and self-consciously working class. Most of them lived with their parents into their twenties and thirties and even beyond. Few owned automobiles. Kirmser's was their only free space, the only place where they could escape the restrictions of their lives. It contrasted sharply with the only other gay bar in the Twin Cities, the Viking Room in the Radisson Hotel in Minneapolis, where the Kirmser's crowd was decidedly uncomfortable. "It was too elegant and too expensive, almost intimidating; waiters wore black pants, black bow ties, short white jackets, and they expected big tips." Mr. and Mrs. Kirmser, although straight, were like their customers, plain working-class people. They struggled to survive in their unattractive little bar, stoically accepting the patronage of those regarded by others as outcasts.

The Evening Crowd at Kirmser's is also about St. Paul at a particular point in its history. It vividly portrays not just

Kirmser's, but other long-gone St. Paul institutions—the Ryan Hotel, the Golden Rule department store, the old Italian neighborhood on the Flats. To a reader a half-century later, what is perhaps most striking is how separate St. Paul was from Minneapolis. Brown and his friends had no sense of being part of a Twin Cities metropolitan area. They were St. Paulites. They rarely went to Minneapolis and when they did they saw it as an alien place—more middle-class, slightly pretentious, less down-to-earth. In the two decades to follow, shared sports teams, metropolitan television stations, the I-94 freeway, and the Metropolitan Council would blur the distinctions between the Twin Cities. But it had not yet happened in 1946.

The St. Paul setting is important in another way, too. Most of our knowledge of gay and lesbian life in the first half of the twentieth century is based on studies of our largest and most cosmopolitan cities—particularly New York and San Francisco. *The Evening Crowd at Kirmser's* provides an unusual glimpse of gay life in a middle-sized, provincial city among ordinary working-class people. It takes its place along with *Boots of Leather, Slippers of Gold,* Elizabeth Lapovsky Kennedy and Madeline Davis's study of the lesbian community in Buffalo, as an important step toward a fuller understanding of the themes and variations in early twentieth-century gay American life.

The Evening Crowd at Kirmser's is a memoir, written years later than the events that it describes. Here it differs from another important gay document from the early twentieth century— the diary of Jeb Alexander, portions of which have been published as *Jeb and Dash: A Diary of Gay Life, 1918–1945* (1993). Jeb Alexander is the pseudonym for a gay man who lived in Washington, D.C., held a routine government job, and every day wrote entries in a diary that he never expected anyone else to read. Jeb's life was more middle-class in its orientation and interests than the lives of Ricardo Brown and his friends, but the demands of closetry were similar. Jeb's circle countered the hostilities and fears they faced daily by seeking friendship and consolation in each other's company.

Much of the authenticity of *Jeb and Dash* derives from its lack of self-consciousness, the fact that it is a private journal written at the time the events it describes occurred. A document like *The Evening Crowd at Kirmser's,* on the other hand, raises questions about memory. Written years later, when Ricardo Brown was an older and wiser man, its interpretations are undoubtedly filtered through subsequent experience. All of our memories of the events of our youth have been skewed by what we have done since and who we have become. Brown lived on into the age of gay liberation and was at least casually involved in some of the struggles of that era. His own fight to receive an honorable discharge from the navy finally succeeded in the changed environment of the 1980s. How Brown saw the events of the 1940s and how he remembered his own reactions to those events must inevitably have been influenced by what he witnessed in his later life. But that is the nature of all memoirs, in fact of memory itself.

Kennedy and Davis's *Boots of Leather, Slippers of Gold* bears comparison with *The Evening Crowd at Kirmser's.* Drawing upon the oral histories of forty-five women from the 1930s until the 1960s, *Boots of Leather* is far more broadly based than *The Evening Crowd at Kirmser's* and its authors, an academic and a librarian, use the rich source material to develop an interpretation of how working-class lesbian resistance helped pave the way for the gay and lesbian liberation movement of the late twentieth century. Ricardo Brown lets his experiences speak for themselves. But many of his themes are similar—the difficulties of maintaining a sense of community without outside support, the desperate search for love in a world that denied its possibility, and the interplay of class and sexuality among people who were self-consciously working class. For the women of Buffalo, a city like St. Paul in many ways, the bar was as central to their lives as it was to Brown's friends. Much maligned by gay liberationists as an exploitative institution, the gay bar needs to be seen historically—much like the Irish saloon, or the Jewish coffeehouse, or the African American barber shop—as a building block of community, a free space where the sense of camaraderie that later led to liberation was first formed.

In the final analysis, *The Evening Crowd at Kirmser's* will take its place among the vital documents of pre-Stonewall gay history for the perspective it offers of gay working-class life in a provincial American city and for the vigor of its language. Ricardo Brown is a gifted storyteller. His characters come to life with all of their strengths and weaknesses. His descriptions of sex are explicit and earthy. Sexuality, after all, is what sets gay people apart and Brown never flinches from that fact. There is no jargon here, no abstract analysis. Ricardo Brown gives us his life as he remembers it. And we should be grateful that he has.

REFERENCES

Alexander, Jeb. *Jeb and Dash: A Diary of Gay Life, 1918–1945.* Edited by Ina Russell. Boston: Faber and Faber, 1993.

Bérubé, Allan. *Coming Out Under Fire: The History of Gay Men and Women in World War Two.* New York: Free Press, 1990.

Chauncey, George. *Gay New York: Gender, Urban Culture, and the Making of the Gay Male World, 1890–1940.* New York: Basic Books, 1994.

Cory, Donald Webster. *The Homosexual in America: A Subjective Approach.* New York: Greenberg, 1951.

Kennedy, Elizabeth Lapovsky, and Madeline D. Davis. *Boots of Leather, Slippers of Gold: The History of a Lesbian Community.* New York: Routledge, 1993.

The Evening Crowd at Kirmser's

1

Kirmser's

WE NEVER JUST WALKED into Kirmser's, nothing as simple as that. We scouted the terrain first to see who might be watching us. If the coast was clear, we stepped forward quickly, yanked the door open and lunged inside, head down, moving toward the cover of a booth or the safety of a bar stool out of range of that small, oblong window in the front.

If there were too many people on the street or too many cars, we might walk right past Kirmser's, as if we didn't know it existed, down to the corner, then double back and, if the coast was clear, we'd duck inside. Once in a while, when pedestrians seemed to be gawking about or if a car looked familiar, like the big, old Packard of Mike's parents or my uncle's Ford, I would even circle the whole block before coming back to Kirmser's to try my entry again.

Kirmser's was the underground queer bar in St. Paul, a hidden sanctuary for homosexual men and women in the 1940s. It was the haven I found in 1945 after I was drummed out of the navy for being a homosexual. I was eighteen years old then and had only been in the navy for six months.

Kirmser's was long, narrow, and deep, like a tunnel. There were no windows save for one oblong window in the front, just big enough for a small, red neon "Liquor" sign, and there was a square window in the front door, no bigger than a book, a necessary precaution to prevent those coming and going from slamming the door into one another.

There was a dark, heavy wooden bar running along one wall, and a faded shuffleboard game painted on the asphalt tile floor up front to one side of the entrance. The jukebox at the back, its glorious, revolving colors of red, blue, and green, pulsating with the music, bubbling through great loops of transparent coils, was a joyful sight in marked contrast to the rest of the place, like a dancing girl in a roomful of nuns.

There were a few old wooden tables and chairs in the center of the room, and along the wall opposite the bar there were creaky, old-fashioned, high-backed varnished booths that had turned black with age.

The plumbing was in the back: a dingy kitchen to the left, where the noon soups were prepared, and the toilets to the right. The men's toilet was cramped, windowless, and antiquated, with a rusty wall-hung trough urinal and a single exposed stool in one dark corner. It reeked of urine, a violent, bottled-up, acidic stench that attacked the eyes and nose when the door was opened.

Kirmser's had no particular decor and it made no pretensions to style. In the winter it was often drafty and chilly; there was no storm door and the heavy wooden front door opened directly into the cold. In the summer, a heavy old electric fan up front moved the dead air around, but on hot, humid nights, sweaty customers in the booths stuck to the old varnish like flies on flypaper.

Kirmser's was located downtown, at 382 Wabasha Street. It was seldom a busy place, except during the Winter Carnival. Drab, utilitarian, and uncomfortable, Kirmser's was the only place we had, though it wasn't exclusively ours. We shared it with a daytime crowd. Kirmser's was a workingman's bar, straight in the daytime and queer at night. Its daytime customers were day laborers, cabdrivers, old clerks, pensioners, railroad men, and a few tough old barflies who found the dim, quiet interior restful and the prices reasonable. Both daytime and nighttime customers had much in common: the same poor jobs, the same limited educations, the same religions, the same family values, even the same neighborhoods.

Our crowd, however, was generally younger, and even if the daytime customers looked in on the night crowd, it was not likely that they would see any obvious differences in us; they wouldn't realize that these ordinary-looking young men and women, nursing their beers, were what they would likely call sexual monsters, perverts who practiced unspeakable "crimes against nature."

Still, we didn't like to take chances. We usually avoided sitting out in the open at the center tables, exposed to any lurking dangers beyond that one small window. We preferred the privacy of the booths. People sitting by themselves at the bar, easier to see by anyone walking past, usually, almost instinctively, sat at an angle with their backs toward that small front window.

The daytime crowd usually got off work and went home to supper and settled in for an evening of listening to Amos 'n' Andy, the Lux Radio Theater, and Kate Smith singing "When the Moon Comes over the Mountain." If they did go out for the evening, to a movie, a beer joint, or a bowling alley, it was usually in their own neighborhood or at least their own part of town. Few working people wanted to get dressed up to come back downtown at night.

The evening crowd at Kirmser's dressed like everyone else, the men with our hair clipped short, sometimes in a military-cut heinie, clean shaven, in baggy but pressed slacks, cotton or rayon shirts, wool sweaters, loafers and wing-tip brogues. The women wore slacks—dressing in slacks was no longer unusual for women since many had begun wearing them to factory jobs during the war—and blouses and low-heeled shoes, their hair cut short, but thicker and longer than ours, and usually curlier. The girls in Kirmser's, the lesbians, spurned makeup, although a couple of the girls who considered themselves femmes wore bright red lipstick and painted their fingernails the same vivid shade.

The Kirmsers themselves were a respectable, older couple of German descent, sober and industrious, plain, dark, and substantial, like good bock beer. Mrs. Kirmser was stout, short, cheerful, and efficient, always dressed in a dull black dress and apron like the Italian widows I knew from the Levee, who wore mourning black from the day their husbands died until the day they died.

She waited tables and, when time allowed, she seemed to enjoy talking to some of us. We liked Mrs. Kirmser, and some of the older guys, like Clem, Lou, and Pete, even took the liberty of calling her "Kitty."

Mr. Kirmser rarely talked to anyone. He was not tall as much as erect, rigid, a dour, square-faced, stern-looking, and aloof old man, a pillar of salt, hiding behind a thick, gray, old-fashioned handlebar moustache. He tended bar, mixed drinks, stocked the beer cooler, carried in the ice, and hauled out the empty bottles. He did not encourage conversation. During lulls in business, he would read his newspaper. He kept his distance from us, always safely behind that moustache, the great barrier of a bar, and his copy of the *Pioneer Press*.

He always seemed to be working in profile, looking out that little front window or looking back into the darkened kitchen. Even when he was waiting on customers at the bar, he seemed to be working sideways, looking off into the distance. It was as if he never wanted to come full face with the type of people who frequented and supported his establishment.

Kirmser's was known to queers as far away as Chicago, but most straight people and even some homosexuals in St. Paul were unaware of it. Those straight people who might know about it, like people who worked in the neighborhood or who patronized the popular Gallivan's bar on the same block, preferred to ignore it. Kirmser's was not the kind of place most people, even straight people, cared to admit too much knowledge of.

Strangers, neither queer nor part of the daytime crowd, occasionally wandered into Kirmser's at night, but they never seemed to suspect anything and, since the place often seemed dull, even standoffish to outsiders, they never stayed long enough to find anything out. If some of our conversations got a little loud or a little careless when one of these strangers was present, Mrs. Kirmser would "Shoosh" the offender, adding a curt warning nod toward the straight customer nearby. We always enjoyed these little acts of conspiracy on Mrs. Kirmser's part, her willing participation in the ruse that kept all of us safe.

Kirmser's was a ma-and-pa operation. Mr. and Mrs. Kirmser put in long hours six days a week. They opened late morning, cleaned up from the night before, put on the noon soup, and made the coffee, then worked straight through until closing at 1 A.M. every day except Saturday, when state blue laws dictated a midnight closing, the minute the Sabbath began.

The Kirmsers never advertised and there was never a hint in any publication that a place like Kirmser's even existed. Homosexuality was rarely acknowledged at that time, and the word itself wasn't usually admitted to public print. Once in a while someone would pencil in a small, discreet message like "69 at Kirmser's Bar" over a urinal at the Greyhound bus depot, but that was the only advertising the place ever got. Gay men and lesbians didn't seem to exist in the public psyche until, as my friend Flaming Youth once observed, "they catch us with the meat in our mouths."

As shocking as Kirmser's would have beeen to the rest of the world, to us it was a refuge, a fort in the midst of a savage and hostile population. Still, it wasn't the only bar in town that catered to queer folks; there was one other outpost in our territory, the Viking Room in the Radisson Hotel across the river in downtown Minneapolis. It was an elegant bar that attracted what Lulu Pulanski called a "more cosmopolitan crowd," a mixture of affluent queers and straights. A few of us from Kirmser's who had made a pilgrimage to the Viking Room did not like it at all, despite its polished oak beams and the handsome, antique Viking murals. It was too elegant and too expensive, almost intimidating; waiters wore black pants, black bow ties, short white jackets, and they expected big tips.

My friend Pete said the place was full of "ribbon clerks," fashionable and pretentious faggots who worked for peanuts in Dayton's department store next door, bored-looking fellows who sat around in vested suits and Countess Mara neckties, drinking martinis and gossiping about the latest antics of Mae West as if they actually knew her. Pete had impressed me by actually identifying a Countess Mara necktie just by looking at the design and he let me think that was the case until he finally told me the truth.

"Shit, she puts her initials on the front of the tie like a price tag," he said, indignant at such silly pretensions. It was still a revelation to me; I didn't know ties were designed in the first place.

No, the Viking Room was too high-class for us. Our territory was Kirmser's, and some of the toilets of St. Paul: the busy basement men's room in the Golden Rule department store; the second-floor toilet in the Bremer Arcade across the street, its massive, old, porcelain, floor-length urinals big enough to stand in; the Midway Montgomery Ward; the men's lounge in the Garrick double-feature theater, its upper facade still showing what was left of the once grand opera house, but its interior darkened and gutted of any former elegance. We also had the Greyhound bus depot, and after-hours cruising at the Coney Island.

In the summertime, we branched out into nearby Rice Park, a flat, square city block of fenced-in concrete and grass. It was enclosed by imposing neighbors. There was the brown brick St. Paul Hotel on one side, a red brick office building opposite, and stationed on the other sides were the public library—a white marble mausoleum in the long and low Italian Renaissance style—and its ornate partner across the way—the massive gray towers, peaks, and cupolas of the federal building, looking like a misplaced Rhine castle.

Kirmser's, by comparison, was the safest and most decent place we had. Toilets were known as "tea rooms" and tea room cruising was frowned on by most of the guys in Kirmser's. Lucky could not understand how anyone could have the "nerve" to do it, and many of us found it degrading and dangerous to size people up as you stood side by side at urinals; that kind of activity was indulged in by men like Flaming Youth and Betty Boop, men for whom the urge to have sex outweighed the fear of discovery, the possibility of arrest.

Still, despite these differences, we all felt that we were comrades of sorts. We all faced the same social stigma, the same threats to our freedom and even our lives. We were all outcasts, what Flaming Youth sardonically described as "tainted meat."

2

That Old Gang of Mine

*I*T WAS UNTHINKABLE TO TELL ANYONE, family or friends, and especially not family, that you were homosexual. There was no greater horror than having our own families shut us out. We were aliens in our own homes, without history, without ancestors, isolated even from one another. The only point of reference we had was Oscar Wilde, a man destroyed by the public discovery of his homosexuality, a scandal so great that it came down to haunt even people like us half a century later, despite the conspiracy of silence, censorship, and hypocrisy.

My friend Lou told me that homosexuals could be imprisoned for years, institutionalized until "cured." In some countries we were executed, and any of us could be beaten to death if the wrong people got wise to us. Although it was unthinkable to let anyone know the truth, I did the unthinkable. After I admitted my homosexuality and was discharged from the navy as "undesirable," I tried to explain the situation to some friends from high school. I reasoned that I wasn't such a bad guy, so why not face it? It was all a matter of public record now anyway, if anyone ever wanted to find out.

The confession made my friends uncomfortable. One of them, who had vowed undying friendship in his yearbook inscription, who took half a page to write in bold letters "You can always count on me," panicked and actually tried to hide from me. He ducked into a doorway, cowering in the far corner, the next time he saw me coming down Main Street. I realized then that I had placed them in an awkward and potentially dangerous situation. I had made them unwilling conspirators. Most of them wanted no part of it.

Only Mike and Harrison acknowledged it. Mike, an odd mixture of German thoroughness and Irish whimsy, demanded to know if I'd told my parents. Mike liked my dad. When he came by the house to see me he'd sometimes stay a while to bullshit with the Old Man. Mike was the short, pudgy brother of two tall, handsome older brothers who played football. Mike played the piano. He loved a good argument and my dad enjoyed this brash, young opponent.

Mike would take an opposing position just to keep an argument going, sometimes even going to the extreme of supporting the policies of President Roosevelt, a man my father detested.

"He's no president; he's a dictator," my father fumed. "He'll be president until the day he dies, buying votes and telling lies, the conniving, blue-balled, harebrained, pig-fucking bastard."

No, my father did not like Franklin Delano Roosevelt. He had voted for Roosevelt twice, thinking he was the man who might lead us out of the Great Depression, but when Roosevelt ran for an unprecedented third term and for yet an unbelievable fourth term, my father was outraged—not speechless but a little incoherent—at such abuse of power. In frustration, he cut out a full-page, colored rotogravure portrait of a smiling Roosevelt and pasted it on the inside of our toilet lid.

We couldn't afford an indoor bathroom when I was growing up, but when I was in high school, we tore down our old outhouse and installed a toilet closet in a corner of the basement. "Full of crap, just like Roosevelt," my father would announce as curious neighbors made occasional pilgrimages to witness the Roosevelt toilet, embarrassing Mother, who diligently scrubbed the gray cement area around the toilet to make sure no visitor could fault her housekeeping.

The kitchen was Mother's domain, her workplace during the day, the heart of the house, the place where the week's bread was baked, the dough rising like an enormous plump mushroom above the shiny tin tub. In the evenings, however, when we were all older, the kitchen table was often littered with my father's newspapers and books, his coffee cup and Bull Durham droppings. Friends of his often dropped in then and the kitchen became a masculine sanctuary, noisy and lively with arguments, challenges, opinions, war stories, town gossip, bad jokes, conflicting versions of history, and graphic descriptions of Franklin Delano Roosevelt. Mother retreated on these evenings to the safety of the dining room, where my sister, Elizabeth, studied and Mother ironed, sewed, mended, and listened to the radio, comfortably close to the brown enamel space heater.

Mike took great stock in being welcomed into that kitchen and he was alert to any possible damage that might come to it.

"Have you told your parents about your discharge?" he asked one day shortly after I'd told him about myself.

"No, I can't tell them that."

He was relieved to hear it.

"Good. They don't deserve a burden like that," he said bluntly.

If Mike was shocked or surprised at my confession, he refused to be thrown off balance by this disclosure. He was as stoic about my being queer as he was about his being short.

Harrison, however, surprised *me.*

Calm, intelligent, reserved, Harrison listened to my confession without comment as we sat on the steps in back of the library one weekend when he was home on furlough from the army.

Well, I finally asked, what do you think?

"It's like you just opened a door in my mind," he said slowly, almost balancing each word as he said it.

"A door?"

"Yes, the same door you came through."

Harrison? My best friend. A queer like me? I could hardly believe it. Harrison, who was so smart he could become president, was a queer like me.

We'd been friends since kindergarten. If I was brash, loud, impulsive, quick to anger, a daydreamer, Harrison never wasted words, knew exactly what to say when he did speak, and possessed an infuriating patience—and success—in solving problems. He refused to say anything rather than speak in anger.

Both our families lived in cheap "company houses" on the North Hill, houses built for the old lumberjacks. Our fathers sometimes found work, but usually didn't. Though we lived in different neighborhoods, we both went to the Garfield school.

Summers we roamed the fields behind my house, and one day while smoking Indian weed, I accidentally set the field on fire. It burned rapidly, making odd, greedy, whipping sounds as it beat its way out past Rock Pond right up to Pearsons' barn, where neighbors rushed in to help put it out. Harrison and I became blood brothers after that. I knew I could trust him. He would never tell on me.

I could count on Mike and Harrison, and I was lucky that in spite of my rashness and confusion, a few other friendships also survived. Still, I never mentioned the word *homosexual* to my straight friends again. We carried on as if nothing of the kind had ever been said, as if nothing of the kind had ever existed, as if I had never been in the navy, as if I had never spoken.

When I was a kid, I'd fooled around with Jim and Orville, two of the bigger boys at the Garfield school. The three of us would sneak off to sheds and ravines to jack off. I marveled at the white, pearly stuff that they were able to squirt out and, encouraged to try it, I discovered it tasted as bitter as library paste. Jizzum, they called it. Pull and yank as hard as I could, I wasn't able to shoot off, but after a few anxious jerks, I felt a marvelous tingle that started at the base of my spine, like electricity, and shot through my legs, and curled my toes.

Once, when Orville's cousin was visiting, we all hiked out to Rock Pond. In the little hollow there, Orville dropped his pants and underwear, lay face down on the hillside, and Jim stuck his cock up Orville's ass.

Orville's cousin dropped his pants and underwear, too, and lay spread out, face down on the hill, grinning back up at me. Nobody said anything about what we were supposed to do, but I knew Orville's cousin was offering himself to me.

I refused. Orville's cousin had eaten a pocketful of green apples earlier in the day, and had taken a dump in the field on the way out to the pond. Now his backside, even his underwear, was smeared with shit.

Jim, seeing my hesitation, pushed himself up slightly off of Orville and hissed at me.

"G'WAN!"

"No," I said, hesitating because I didn't want to get anywhere near Orville's soiled cousin, but afraid because I didn't want Jim to think I was a sissy. "It's dirty."

"Aw, G'WAN," Jim coaxed while he continued to pump Orville's ass.

Not me. I wasn't going to stick anything of mine into something like that. On the way back home, because I hadn't been a good sport, the others walked ahead of me through the tall grass. They wouldn't talk to me, so I followed forlornly behind, clearly no longer part of the gang.

For a long time I thought maybe that was why everything changed. Jim and Orville were in junior high school now and there were no more field trips, no more meetings in the shed, no more jizzum. I jerked off by myself.

I finally discovered that the two of them had rocketed into a whole new world, leaving me behind. They had taken off like Buck Rogers from Planet Earth, and flown to an alien world, a world of Girls.

Once, when I tagged along with them from the skating rink, Jim bragged about playing "stink finger" with a girl named Ellen, and they both smirked. I thought it was a horrible way to talk about a girl.

Though something had gone wrong between Orville and Jim and me, I knew now that IT was out there. IT did exist. I had to keep looking and once I found it, everything would be like Shangri-la, a secret, loyal brotherhood as wonderful as the Masons or the Odd Fellows or the Knights of Columbus.

Instead, when I got into high school, I found Swivel Hips. "Swivel Hips" is what I heard some high school boys call him. God, the way he walked, who could miss him? We'd meet in the basement toilet of the Carnegie library, a bare, hot cell with a sink and a toilet, and we'd lock ourselves in for a few frantic moments. He was in college on a scholarship and he had learned things there that the good citizens of Stillwater, my hometown, would never understand.

He told me about a neighborhood in New York called Greenwich Village, a place full of what he called "joy boys," men like him and me. Anxious that I should properly understand everything associated with our own kind, the still mysterious world we inhabited, he also told me that the proper word for people like us was *homosexual*. From the Latin, he explained.

Latin? The language we chanted and sang at Mass? What had I missed? Was Latin the answer? Was Latin the clue? I eagerly took Latin my last two years in high school, the attentive student of Miss Flandreau. I learned that Latin was the father of French, Italian, and Spanish—the "Romance languages." I perked up at the romance angle, hoping that my teacher might have something enlightening and illicit to share, but Miss Flandreau let her explanation drop at that, and I was left hanging. Still, she taught fervently, even passionately, indignant at the smallest sign of indifference among us, any slight carelessness in pronunciation.

"You don't know one iota about today's lesson," she would declare on days when she felt we weren't doing our best. "It's appalling."

There she stood, an imperious presence, the guardian of a lost civilization. How dull mathematics and science seemed, taught by instructors who were merely educated. Miss Flandreau was not only educated, people agreed, she was *cultured*.

However, she never solved my problem. I was ashamed of what Swivel Hips and I did, but silly as he was, he had given me one key to the world. It wasn't Latin, of course. It was Greenwich Village.

I made a beeline for Greenwich Village the minute I graduated from high school, seventeen years old and my graduation money tucked into my first billfold. I hopped a Greyhound bus in St. Paul and ended up, a few days later, in New York City.

I had no plans for when I arrived. I only knew I had to get to New York. It was where people like me, even like Swivel Hips, lived. I expected to find the whole city alive with people like me, dancing in the streets, my own kind—you know, joyful and triumphant—and riding the Greyhound bus, dozing on and off in my seat, I dreamed vague and beautiful dreams of a welcoming band meeting my bus, of going to the theater, of gay parties and candlelight dinners, of being swept off my feet by some prince, a writer or an artist or an actor, someone as fine as Bud York, a boy I had dreamed of and lusted after in high school.

I walked out of the bus depot, carrying my family's old suitcase, disappointed at the obvious indifference I found, but dazzled by the energy and the variety of the city, the bright lights, the rushing, determined people, the streets lined with endless restaurants and bars and curious little places called delicatessens.

I found a tiny furnished room, a hall bedroom, in a musty old brownstone on Perry Street. I had arrived in the Village.

Four days later, I met my first "joy boy." He was sitting beside me on a stool at the soda fountain in the village drugstore.

"Am I being rather obvious?" he murmured as he offered to pay for my egg salad sandwich. He certainly was no boy, not by a long shot, and he wasn't too joyful either. He was slim, dark, and rather solemn looking, and he smelled strongly of something that wasn't aftershave. I suspected it was perfume.

He was an entertainer, he told me, the master of ceremonies at a nightclub. He invited me to come see the show and he gave me a pass that I could give to the doorman. Afterward, he offered, we could go out for something to eat.

When I arrived at his nightclub that evening, I found an ugly, foul-smelling little bar. As I settled into a seat at a tiny table far back in the corner where the waiter had discreetly placed me, I found myself seated next to an army sergeant in full uniform, his chest full of battle ribbons. I wasn't sure if I was seeing right because the place was so dark, but it looked like the master sergeant was holding hands with a willowy blond fellow seated beside him.

I only saw one woman in the place—a mean-looking, big-shouldered blond in a tan jacket—and she looked more military than the sergeant. She was seated like an eagle, attended by three giggling male sparrows.

Before I had a chance to check back on the sergeant, the house lights dimmed, a bright spotlight wavered, then found the tiny stage, and a record began playing "A Pretty Girl Is Like a Melody." My date for the evening, the master of ceremonies, burst through the curtains. He was dressed in a black tuxedo and his face was thick with pancake makeup. He very ceremoniously opened the show. I had never been to a gay nightclub before. I had no idea what to expect.

For a few seconds, as the performers first stalked onto the stage, I thought the show was a comedy. After all, the performers were all men dressed as women. Slowly, however, it became clear to me that this wasn't a joke at all. There was something deadly serious about this masquerade. The men all wore long dresses, high-heeled shoes, elaborate wigs, and fake jewelry. Their faces were painted in bold, primary colors like the Sunday funny papers, with glowing red lipstick, blue or green eye shadow, black mascara, powdered and rouged faces of all colors. There was something vivid about them, almost exciting, except for their eyes. Their eyes were not alive, but blank, cold, and glittering, hard as steel; they were ball-bearing eyes, machines that measured and challenged every member of the audience.

The performers promenaded and posed, even sang in crude imitation of women. They were men with thick fingers, husky voices, and awkward strides, the more noticeable when they tried to be graceful. It was as if they had been disemboweled, gutted, nothing either masculine or feminine remaining. They were curious, almost feral creatures who were on exhibition, but they had somehow craftily turned the tables on their keepers, and it was impossible to know who was watching whom. With a shake of the hips, a coy shrug of the shoulders, a knowing leer, a coarse gesture, a dirty joke, each of them in turn put the audience through our paces, and we responded on cue with shrieks of glee, raucous laughter, and prolonged, automatic applause, clapping our hands like trained seals when commanded.

"Come on now, let's hear it. How about a big hand for Billie LeClair!"

And the beasts in the audience obeyed.

When the house lights came back on and I could see to make my escape, I dodged awkwardly between the closely packed tables and bolted out the door into freedom, greedily gulping in the sweet, pure, New York night air.

I knew I wasn't like those people. I might not know who I was, or what, but I wasn't like them; I couldn't be. Why had that man invited me here? Was my master of ceremonies trying to tell me something? Was this a look into the future?

The night air was colder now. I shivered a little.

I was disillusioned. I had come to New York expecting to find myself, and all I found was a fey master of ceremonies and a seedy nightclub where costumed men made a mockery of everything I'd been told was masculine, where everything I knew of the world was turned on its head. A few days later, tired, shell-shocked, and ready to admit defeat, I left New York. When the bus pulled into the St. Paul Greyhound depot a few days later, I realized how good it was to be back in Minnesota, even if there weren't many joy boys to be found, and certainly no female impersonators.

Just before my eighteenth birthday, as my dad suggested, I enlisted in the navy. My dad had fought in what his generation thought was the War to End All Wars, but it hadn't turned out that way. His war hadn't prevented my war, and all he could do now was advise me that the navy offered a cleaner tour of duty than a soldier could find crawling around in the mud on your belly in the army.

My first week in boot camp, I became the best buddy of a bunkmate named Bliss. There was something special about him, something that made me anxious to win his approval. I thought that, after Jim and Orville, after Swivel Hips and the female impersonators in Greenwich Village, this was it. Bliss was the Promised Land, someone who might like me, even love me, someone who willingly slept beside me, showered with me, shared cigarettes, traded comic books and cookies from home, ate breakfast, lunch, and supper with me, borrowed my stamps and my toothpaste, came with me to the canteen, told me jokes, exchanged confidences about our hometowns.

We shared everything, almost like a good marriage. I eagerly got up in the morning, anxious to spend all the time I could with him. He had small ears, a hard head, and small black eyes, and I would have punched anyone who suggested that he was a little bit bucktoothed. He looked innocent but he *smelled* naked, not in the noisy cattle commotion of the showers, but at night when I watched him sleep, an arm's length away, warm, vulnerable, curled like a child, his white boxer shorts tightly wrapped around his hips, his bare chest as white and smooth as Ivory soap, his mouth slightly open, perfectly at peace. I would finally fall asleep to dream of white angels, as naked and beautiful as Bliss.

Buddies at first, even a little goosey with each other (which had falsely raised my hopes), he brushed me off when he finally guessed what I was up to. Had he caught me watching him sleep? I suppose that would give anyone a spooky feeling. I must have seemed like a vampire, studying him, lying in wait, longing to sink my teeth anywhere into that bare, ivory skin.

He soon paired up with some guy named Steele who bunked at the other end of the barracks. They became bosom buddies, like Bliss and I once were. They went to chow together, jaunted off to the canteen, washed their clothes together, huddled together during their free time in the barracks. Bliss turned his back to me now when he fell asleep. He acted as if I didn't exist.

Jim and Orville, Swivel Hips, the female impersonators, and Bliss. Then there was the drunken ensign I met on leave in Chicago. One stupid mistake, one calamity, one dead end after another. Bliss and Steele had shipped out after boot camp to serve on the buddy ship, while I was tapped for yeoman school. I soon sunk into a world so strange that not even Buck Rogers could find me.

I cut classes. I roamed the base all day, often spending hours sitting in the cab of some big earth-moving machine that sat abandoned in a deserted corner of the base. Instead of going to yeoman classes, after breakfast I'd hike over to the construction site and climb up into the cab and sit. I don't think anyone ever missed me. I was no longer sure that I would recognize my own Shangri-la, even if I found it. I felt like I had the ticket in my hand, but I kept getting on the wrong buses.

I disappeared into some wasteland, a deep pit that I wasn't sure I wanted to get out of. There was no heaven above, but I knew I wasn't in hell. I was in limbo. I had stumbled into a void, that Catholic dimension that is neither hell nor heaven, a place where nothing, not even time, exists.

When I finally noticed a dim flicker of light at the edge of the void, I wasn't sure if I had the energy or even the desire to try to reach it. But I crawled up the steep side of that pit and stood at the top of it, then moved slowly toward the beckoning light.

When I reached the light, I stepped into its blinding clarity and stood before my chief petty officer, and in a language so foreign and mysterious to him that he could only gape at me in amazement, I announced, "Sir, I am homosexual."

Months later, after I'd met Lucky, he lectured me about the dangers of my brash decision. *You could lose your job if people found out about you. Your family might throw you out. You couldn't trust anyone.* He was right. Even once I found Kirmser's, I knew I couldn't fully trust anyone there. An anonymous letter or phone call, motivated by hate, spite, jealousy, or revenge, accusing you of being queer, could destroy you.

My friend Dale had been fired from an office job he'd had for six years with Central Coal and Oil Company after a call like that to his boss. Called into his boss's office, Dale picked up the piece of paper that his boss had pushed across the desk with the backs of his fingers, as if afraid to soil his hands.

The note read, "You got a cocksucker working for you. His name's Dale."

"I don't know who called and I don't care," his boss said. "That's what the caller said. I don't want to hear anything like that ever again. I want you out of here this morning. Irene will mail you your check."

Dale was out the door and out of a job that same morning, and he spent the afternoon in the Garrick Theater, hiding in the dark, slumped down in his seat, sick to his stomach, sure he would never get another job and panicked at the thought of having to go home and tell his mother that he had lost his job.

A job was a sacred thing, something that all of us who were brought up in the depression knew was hard to come by, something that you stayed with until you died or went blind.

Dale lived at home, like most of us, with his mother and a kid sister who was disabled after a bout with polio. His mother and sister doted on Dale, looked after him. "They spoil me rotten," Dale said, ashamed now that he might not be able to take care of them.

Dale told his mother that he had been laid off because business was slow. It was a stupid lie; how could business be slow when the company sold coal in Minneapolis in the winter? Dale's married brother, a big shot with the state, finally got Dale a job at the capitol, but most of us, if anything like that happened, did not have an influential relative to fall back on.

We didn't always trust one another at Kirmser's, but we did have a feeling of kinship. We had been brought up in stable, family-oriented, religious homes, and we tried to apply the values we learned there to the small brotherhood and sisterhood at Kirmser's. We might be jealous of one another, suspicious, even hateful at times, but there was no denying our blood bond. We were family.

Not that we didn't have our pecking order, just like the rest of the world. We divided the dykes into two simple groups, butch and femme, but it was a more complicated structure for the men.

Sissies were near the bottom of the heap, whether they were tough little whores like Betty Boop, or sensitive souls like Dickie Grant and Mother Jerusalem. Running slightly ahead of the sissies were phonies or elegant bitches, the piss elegant type. We had one of those. We called him Lulu. At the very bottom of the heap were "aunties," old farts like the Edstrom brothers, sissies too old to be merely sissies anymore, but something more tenacious, though less desirable. The Edstrom brothers were our resident old aunties. They had tried their damnedest to be elegant and grand, but they had moved from sissy to old auntie without ever making it, even briefly, into the piss elegant class.

At the top of the list were the Regular Guys like Lucky, Bart, Red Larson, Chester, Dale, Mick Flaherty, and Tom Clark. There also was an older Regular Guy group that included Pete and Ned, John the librarian, the quietest guy I had ever met, and Lou, who worked for West Publishing.

Nicknames were common at Kirmser's. Betty Boop loved his. He thought it was cute, being named after an adorable little cartoon character, curly-haired and saucer-eyed. Lulu Pulanski didn't like to be called "Lulu," but he was careful not to make a fuss about it for fear it could get worse. Mother Jerusalem was never aware of his nickname, and I never heard anyone call him that to his face. He was a young, plump, Jewish fellow, as pleasant as he was homely. He had a big Jewish nose, "full of nickels," like my uncle always said, with curly golden hair and a good job in his uncle's jewelry store. He was always so sympathetic, so polite and good-natured, so careful about things, so motherly.

People like Flaming Youth, Bud York, and Clem Haupers, the old artist, were in a class by themselves.

Flaming Youth was the most notorious queer in the city, a legend almost, a man who, the story went, could turn tricks even during his noon hour. Flaming Youth, whose real name was Joe, was in his forties, bald with a large droopy gray moustache and bags under his eyes, but he was still referred to as Flaming Youth, the name the Edstrom brothers had bestowed on him when he first came out, wild and rambunctious, years ago during the Roaring Twenties.

We were all a little in awe of Clem Haupers, even as old and paunchy as he was, not only because he actually made a living as an artist, but because he was the only one of us who was able to carry on a conversation with Mr. Kirmser.

Bud York was a queer's dream; there was nobody in the world like him. Pete, who always liked to pin tags on people, and not always nice ones, called Bud "The All-American Boy"—and he meant it.

Bud York was not just a Regular Guy. He was a Greek god, cocksure, tall, young, butch, and good-looking, with a boyish enthusiasm and all the right credentials. He never showed any of the doubts, guilt, or inferiority that sometimes plagued the rest of us. He had confidence as smooth and hard as granite, and nothing could penetrate it or stick to it.

He had been a high school football player, a lieutenant in the army, and now he had a good job as an insurance salesman.

"I'll bet when he gets a hard-on a cat couldn't scratch it," Pete had once remarked, an unusual tribute from someone who was not ordinarily inclined to pass out compliments.

Bud had gone to high school in Stillwater, my hometown, for a couple of years before his family moved back to St. Paul. He was six years older than I was, and I'd had a crush on him one summer when I was eleven or twelve; I'd watch him swimming and showing off at St. Croix beach.

When he showed up in Kirmser's, I could hardly believe it. Bud York in Kirmser's? Bud York *one of the boys*? He remembered me from Stillwater and he asked me out. Bud York and me. Holy shit! I was in Seventh Heaven, on Cloud Nine, Dancing on the Stars. It was just like the movies.

Most of us had few illusions, but we all had our standards and our pride.

Lou, one of the older "Regular Guys" at Kirmser's, had been ready to take care of a young fellow in the Garrick toilet one afternoon, when he peeled back the man's foreskin and shot right back up to his feet.

"Do you ever wash that thing?" he demanded. "You do your part and I'll do my part—like the NRA."

I laughed at Lou harking back to the notorious NRA, Roosevelt's pet National Recovery Act. It had been declared unconstitutional by the Supreme Court, a power that even Roosevelt couldn't control. Still, it had once offered the working class a great rallying cry. Even my father had pasted the big blue eagle emblem, NRA, with the famous slogan, "We Do Our Part," in our front window in the days before he had consigned Roosevelt to the toilet. I never thought it could apply to the business that went on in the Garrick toilet.

3

The Promised Land

WHEN I FIRST FOUND KIRMSER'S, I couldn't believe it. A queer bar in St. Paul? I was astonished when Red Larson and Chester finally told me about it. I knew there were queer bars in cities like New York—I'd been to one— but I never dreamed a place like that could exist in St. Paul.

I'd met Red and Chester at work, when I took a part-time job three nights a week in the circulation department of the *Pioneer Press* after my discharge from the navy. Red was a blustery, chubby guy who seemed to have just two expressions: a jolly, anxious-to-please look, and a scarlet stare, glassy-eyed and guilty whenever he felt threatened or cornered. He seemed like an odd companion for the quiet, reserved Chester, but they were good friends, bachelors, both army veterans and both very friendly. Their attentions to me seemed natural enough; St. Paul was a friendly town.

I was working full time as a shipping clerk, but I had taken on the night job at the *Pioneer Press* to earn extra money, and to escape from the confines of my family and my home a few nights a week. My mother and father knew something was wrong with my sudden discharge from the navy, but I wouldn't talk about it. I'd hidden my yellow undesirable discharge papers under the linoleum flooring beneath my bed, not knowing what else to do with them. I was afraid to destroy the document because it looked so official, but I couldn't take the chance that either of my parents would discover it.

I told them only that I had a medical discharge because of pleurisy. It was partly true; I'd been hospitalized with pleurisy in the midst of being discharged as homosexual, but I didn't carry off the lie very well. When friends or relatives dropped by our house now to talk about the war, I had nothing to say. My father, who loved to talk, often just listened. His war had been the First World War. He had been a marine in what he had once believed was the Great War, the War to End All Wars, the war to make the world safe for democracy. The Great War. How romantic it sounded, how classic, as glorious and noble as the Crusades. Now, with the advent of the Second World War, it had become just a prelude to the current catastrophe. I avoided those kitchen get-togethers, often taking the late bus home so that my folks were in bed by the time I got back. I had nothing to say about war.

I'd found the shipping clerk job right away, claiming I was 4-F because of a punctured eardrum. That's what kept Frank Sinatra out of the war, and if a punctured eardrum was no handicap to a singer, it couldn't be a drawback to a shipping clerk. Mother, with her native Italian respect for any kind of honest work, was reassured when I found a job, when I got up early each morning to catch the bus from Stillwater to St. Paul, taking the lunch she had packed. She felt nothing could be seriously wrong if I was working for a living. My dad knew better. As a marine wounded in action, he was well acquainted with the machinations of the military. He knew something was wrong, but he never forced the issue. He was willing to wait until I was ready to talk about it.

Chester and Red were not only friendly when they saw me at work, but they also began showing up at Mickey's sandwich shop, where I usually got something to eat before going to the night job. Meg, who worked with me days, sometimes came along, too, for a bowl of soup or chili before she went home to the apartment that she shared with her friend Jill. Meg was good company, a big, cheerful, good-looking Irish girl from North Dakota, well-rounded and perfectly proportioned, quick on her reflexes, sure of her instincts, and light on her feet. She was always immaculate in appearance, with curly, black hair, sparkling dark eyes, and a milkmaid's clear, creamy complexion.

She ran the ditto machine for the company, a job not much better than mine, and she did it with as much care as if she were typing the president's letters. The tan smock she wore when she was working on the machine was always as crisp and clean as a nurse's uniform. I loved to hear her laugh, a country laughter, natural and open-hearted, warm and reassuring, laughter that sometimes made people sitting nearby turn, smiling expectantly, to seek the source of such enjoyment. Her laughter defined her better than anything else, and it set her limits. Her laughter could take on an edge of scorn, of disbelief, if she felt someone was stepping over the line, and even the biggest oaf knew when he was put in his place. Meg loved a good time, but she was nobody's fool.

Meg had a gift of making light of life's disappointments, such as the rancid bean soup we had one night at Mickey's. It was so bad we couldn't eat it, but it became one of those comfortable jokes we shared. "Let's go get some sour bean soup," became her signal for us to hike over to Mickey's for a cheap supper of hamburgers or chili. We steered clear of the bean soup.

I was beginning to wonder about Chester and Red. They finally asked me if Meg was my girlfriend, and when I said no, she's just a friend of mine, a girl I work with, they seemed glad to hear it. There always seemed to be something on their minds that they never mentioned. It wasn't Chester who made me wonder, he was naturally reserved, but Red was something else, forthright, aboveboard, and full of talk. He often seemed on the brink of saying something, then he'd clumsily pull back, his face turning scarlet. I was beginning to suspect what it was when, after a few weeks of fencing around with each other—oblique looks, coy questions about girlfriends, the old army joke about dropping the soap in the shower, comments about how horny a guy can get, about beating your meat—they offered to take me to a "kind of interesting place" some night.

On the way over, they confided that it was a queer bar, and when we stopped at Kirmser's right on Wabasha Street, I thought they were kidding. But there it was, a queer bar, smack in the middle of downtown St. Paul and only a block away from where my Aunt Mary worked. I could not imagine what it would be like, but I figured it couldn't be too bad if Chester went there. My main concern, even overriding my curiosity, was whether I would be able to get in because at age eighteen I was a minor. It was no problem. Mrs. Kirmser greeted Red and Chester pleasantly, took our order, and never questioned me about my age.

Chester and Red began to introduce me around, like a long lost brother, to the few other customers there. My disappointment in the place—it was as drab and plain as the Snow White Sandwich Shop, my old high school hangout in Stillwater—was overcome when I met Dale and Lucky.

Dale and Lucky were nice-looking guys.

"Is Lucky queer?" I asked when we came back to our booth.

"Oh, yeah, he's one of the boys," Red assured me.

"You'd never guess it," I said, and both Red and Chester laughed, delighted at my reactions.

Red plunged right in, eagerly filling in the details, and outlining the possibilities for me.

"Lucky's not going with anybody right now. And Dale just broke up with a guy named Flaherty."

I had my eyes on Lucky, but Chester had plans of his own. He invited me over to his house to spend a Saturday night. We could hang around Kirmser's until closing time and then

go to his house, rather than my catching the last bus out to
Stillwater.

I hadn't counted on Chester asking me out. I hadn't even
considered that possibility. I was still thinking of him and Red
as just friends, a couple of guys I worked with. Chester didn't
appeal to me at all; he was good looking, but he had flat, two-
dimensional good looks, like a nice cameo. There was polish,
but no fire. Still, he was blond.

"Sure, sounds good," I said.

His parents didn't know about him, of course, but we
worked at the same place and I could easily have missed the
last bus to Stillwater. He'd leave a note downstairs in the breakfast nook for his parents to find in the morning so they would
expect us both for breakfast. Although I wasn't attracted to
Chester, I was all for it. He was okay. Red was on the beefy
side, but Chester was okay. Kind of refined, but okay. And I
was curious about how someone that polite would act in bed.

We could have gone to a hotel for the night, but Chester
insisted that we go to his house. He wanted to endow the night
with meaning, some significance, some kind of stability. He
wanted me to meet his parents. He didn't want this to be a
one-night stand.

He had explained all this to me as we drove out to his
house, and even if it sounded corny, I liked him for it. I told
him about my trip to New York, how I'd wanted to carve out a
career as a writer or an artist. I told him about what I'd found
in New York, why I came home, and why I enlisted in the
navy. I told Chester all of this, but I never mentioned my undesirable discharge. I no longer tried to explain it to friends. It
had been a terrible mistake and I didn't want to talk about it.

Chester had his first sexual experience when he enlisted in
the army and was stationed in Germany. He was twenty-five
years old when he and a soldier buddy got drunk one night,
climbed into bed in a hotel room, and masturbated each other.
In the morning, sober and horrified at the night's disclosures,

they both pretended that nothing had happened. After that, although they were in the same outfit, they avoided one another.

Chester grew up believing he was the only boy in the world who felt like he did, who had that peculiar and frightening attraction to other boys. Afraid that he might somehow give himself away, he avoided making friends in high school for fear of being discovered.

"That sounds awful," I said.

"Yes," he replied with an odd, slight smile, the look of someone now safely ashore who looks back with relief and a little embarrassment at his panic when he thought the boat would capsize. "It wasn't very pleasant."

At least I had Orville and Jim to show me the way, as temporary as that was. It was kind of funny, when I thought about it. I had been brought out by two heterosexuals who probably didn't even know their Latin.

Chester woke me the next morning. He was resting on his elbow, at my side, peering down at me with a stricken look on his face. He whispered hoarsely.

"You don't hate me, do you, for what I did last night?"

He looked like he was going to cry.

What was he talking about? Why would I hate him? What had he done that I hadn't done? What had happened to him? How had he changed from the prince of the night before into this morning's frog?

I turned away from those big, guilty eyes. I didn't know where to look; I didn't know what to say. I glanced around the room, the venetian blinds, the striped drapes, the blond furniture—it all matched—the blue carpet on the floor.

We lay there, slightly apart, wary of one another now, he with guilt and me with apprehension, gingerly testing the situation, searching for some kind of safe zone.

I felt rotten and I felt trapped. I knew I had to get the hell out of there.

"I don't hate you," I said, moving out of bed, careful not to touch him. I couldn't even look at him. I just wanted to go home.

But we had to go downstairs to meet his parents.

They were patiently waiting for Junior and his overnight guest, and as we came downstairs, there was the thick, pungent smell of frying bacon, pleasantly familiar and somehow reassuring. The dining room table was set with a cheerful yellow linen cloth and centered with a large silver bowl of fruit. If Chester's parents had any idea what had gone on in Chester's bedroom the night before, they gave no indication. I was uneasy, wondering what they might have heard, the soft sounds, the tense whispers, Chester getting up to go to the toilet. But they were cordial, solicitous even, concealing what curiosity they might have had about me, anxious to please any new friend of their only child.

Chester recovered at breakfast—maybe it was that strong, intoxicating odor of bacon—more confident now in his role as host, and we sat through a pleasant breakfast, talking about movies—we all liked Laurel and Hardy—canoeing on the St. Croix River where Chester's folks had a cottage, and the Winter Carnival, remarking on the size of some of the old ice castles, which were big enough for people to walk through.

"Get lost in even," Chester's father said, smiling at Chester's mother in a way that made me realize this was some kind of family joke because Chester's mother immediately picked up her cue.

"Yes," she said. "F. Scott Fitzgerald infuriated my mother by writing a story called 'The Ice Castle,' where a dainty Southern belle, from Alabama, I believe, visiting St. Paul got lost—frostbitten even—in one of the big, old ice castles. Couldn't find her way out! My mother was from New England and she had no patience with women whom she called clinging vines. She eventually forgave Fitzgerald for writing the story since he was from St. Paul. 'He drinks, you know,' she explained in his defense, a very tolerant attitude for my mother. But she always disliked that foolish Southern girl."

We all laughed, and Chester sat there, bright and attentive, basking in our enjoyment, happy to see us all getting on so well together.

I made an awkward escape almost as soon as we were through eating, glad to be out of there, although Chester apparently had been expecting me to spend the day. It had been, I thought bleakly as Chester drove me back downtown, the shortest honeymoon on record.

4

The All-American Boy

*I*NEVER HAD MUCH TO DO with Chester after that, although we always spoke whenever we met in Kirmser's. We'd buy drinks for one another and I'd ask about his folks and he'd tell me I was looking good.

I got in the habit of stopping in Kirmser's after my night job and hanging around until I had to catch the bus home. It was always pleasant in Kirmser's; it was never busy, but there were always a couple of decent guys to talk to. It was a relief to sneak into the familiar bar and peel off the hypocrisy, lay it aside for a while like shedding a heavy winter coat. We could sit down among friends, people like us, and be ourselves, not having to worry about what we said. Once we stepped back outside, however, back into the reality of Wabasha Street, life became a cold and serious intrigue again. You could never let your guard down. You always had to watch for the signals and the traps.

I learned that lesson early, when I was in high school, and attended a party at my friend Lola's house. When I was in high school I smoked, most of us did, but Lola was the only girl I knew who smoked at home. Just after graduation, Lola decided to host a party, and her parents said that we could all smoke there. We had graduated from high school, and some of us were going to war, so Lola's parents felt we should act like and be treated like adults. For the first time in our lives, we were allowed to smoke in a parents' home, no more sneaking around, no more pretending.

We were all out on the sun porch, a big room her father had built off the kitchen, and I lit a Chesterfield just as Mr. Kobinske came out to say hello. He frowned when he saw me put my Chesterfields back in my coat pocket and exhale. We had all stopped talking, out of deference to his appearance, and now he looked at me with obvious disapproval.

God, what had I done? If he didn't care if we smoked, why was he glaring at me? I had lit my Chesterfield carefully, cupping the match in my hands, like I had seen my father light up his Bull Durham cigarettes, and I had struck the match toward me as I lit up as I knew men were supposed to do. Women, supposedly afraid of fire, struck matches away from themselves. I had observed all of this, had put it all together, the mechanics, the formalities, the codes. I thought I had it all taken care of, but something was wrong.

"What're you smoking Chesterfields for?" Mr. Kobinske demanded. "That's a woman's cigarette. Camels," he said, signaling with his own cigarette, "are a man's smoke."

He shook a Camel loose from his pack and pushed it at me.

I sat there feeling exposed, undone. In the awkward silence, all of my friends were watching me. I thought I had it all taken care of, the right gestures, the man's role, but I had slipped up on the most obvious detail of all. I was smoking a woman's cigarette.

I had no idea why it was, but somehow, in that treacherous jungle of male and female symbols, that great gulf between manhood and sissyhood, Chesterfields were feminine and Camels were masculine. It had never occurred to me that cigarettes—unless they were the obviously sissified filters like Parliaments—were masculine and feminine. Camels were harsh-tasting and strong, with a stupid picture of a camel on the package.

"They taste like camel shit," I later complained. But by the time I enlisted in the navy a few months later, I had switched to Camels.

We always had to keep our guard up. We all learned to get by on lies, deceit, illusions. We were expected to go out with girls, so we dated girls. We double dated with straight friends. No girl ever called our bluff because they were nice girls and nice girls did not try to seduce their boyfriends.

Wanting to keep our friendship as honest as I could, I told Meg that I was "queer." I tried to make my pronouncement as matter-of-fact as I could because I didn't want to frighten her off.

"Queerer than who?" she promptly asked, out-matter-of-facting me, and I knew it was all right. She never treated me any different after that. And after that, I never felt guilty about taking her out.

By then, I was beginning to spend more time in Kirmser's, talking to Lou, Pete, Ned, and Lucky, whom I had gone out with a couple of times.

We were all sitting around a back booth one night when Bud York walked in. He went up to the bar and spoke to Tony, one of the young dykes who apparently knew him. I couldn't believe my eyes. Bud York, the idol of my school days. In Kirmser's. The most beautiful guy in the world. In Kirmser's. He had taken off his topcoat, folded it and placed it on a near-by bar stool as he stood there, posed there almost, in radiant magnificence in his army lieutenant's uniform.

Even Lou, ordinarily the most stoic of us all, was overwhelmed.

"My God," he gasped, "what a splendid sight."

Bud York was smiling, that big, confident grin, carrying on a conversation with Tony as calmly as if they were in Walgreen's drugstore. Bud York, the high school football player, a lieutenant in the army, in Kirmser's.

He must be "one of the boys." It was something right out of the movies, a surprise twist like an O. Henry story.

All one summer I had watched him, fascinated, that last summer of his in Stillwater before his family moved back to St. Paul. I saw him often at the beaches, and a couple of times in the St. Croix drugstore when he and his friends were drinking Cokes.

He was a husky, good-looking guy. He had a broken nose that hadn't healed too well, and it gave him an almost pugnacious look, like a gladiator. Yet, there was nothing of the warrior about him when he smiled, a generous, infectious grin that cracked open his whole face, lighting it up like a bonfire. If Meg's laugh attracted people, Bud York's grin entrapped them.

He was six years older than me and he had been one of the most popular kids in town. Jim and Orville couldn't hold a candle to him. His family lived in one of the old apartment buildings downtown. This was the only odd thing about him. People we knew lived in houses, in real neighborhoods. They had yards and gardens. Grandparents lived with them and sometimes an uncle or an aunt. What kind of family lived in an apartment? Wouldn't you think that they'd want to settle down and get a house of their own?

My family's house was a "company house," one of those built for the lumberjacks who came to the St. Croix Valley to cut the white pine. It was a plain brown, weather-beaten house on a gravel street at the end of town, but it was ours. Grandpa Brown, who had come down from Canada to work in the lumber camps, had bought it.

I saw Bud at the beaches often that summer. I was eleven or twelve years old then, and he was a senior in high school. I'd seen him at Lily Lake, where there was no bathhouse and we had to change back in the weeds, and I'd seen him at the supervised American Legion Beach across the river. Once, when our neighbor, Mr. Fletcher, had loaded up his Model A Ford and taken a bunch of us neighborhood kids, packed in the backseat and riding on the running board, wind-whipped and delighted, all the way to Perch Lake in Wisconsin, Bud York was there.

It was a magical afternoon, riding the running board, bouncing along the country roads, churning up great clouds of dust and hard little pebbles that clattered against the car like buckshot. We were laughing and hollering with excitement, off to the cold, clear beauty of Perch Lake, where tiny fish nibbled at your toes near the sandy bottom. To find Bud York swimming there when we arrived seemed like a blessing. I tried to get as tan as Bud. I was lightly tanned, and skinny. Bud York was as tan as an acorn and strong as an oak.

I never said anything to anybody about Bud York, but I could not understand why all the others, the teachers, his classmates, our parents, anyone who knew him, treated him as if he were ordinary. He was the most magnificent boy in the world. He was so natural at every sport he tried, and he seemed to enjoy himself so much, that I couldn't keep my eyes off him.

He must have been aware, somehow, of my distant hero worship, because that summer, whenever he would pass near me, he'd grin and say "Hi," although I didn't know him and the only way he could have known me was when he'd visit his friends in my neighborhood.

One day that summer, I waited at Legion Beach until Bud had finished swimming and he had run into the old roofless, concrete bathhouse, followed by a couple of his friends. I followed him in, hastily moving my shirt, underpants, and pants over to his area so I could be near him as he took off his bathing suit.

He and his friends were horsing around, all naked, their smooth wet skin glistening and sparkling, bodies burned to a bronze, sometimes scarlet glow from the sun, while their bare, white bottoms, hidden by their bathing suits, were as white and sweet looking as milk.

Jumping in and out of the cold water shower stall in one corner, they pushed, shoved, and elbowed one another, laughing and slapping at each other with their wet wool bathing suits. They were having such a good time I was sure they wouldn't notice me watching them, but in the midst of their horseplay, Bud York glanced over, looked straight at me, and grinned. A tingling, exhilarating sensation rushed up the back of my neck when I realized he had been watching me.

I was so embarrassed at being caught watching him, naked and beautiful as he was, that I frowned, turned my back on him, and clumsily pulled on my clothes. I hastily left the building and started the long walk back home. It was a route that took me across the bridge, through downtown Stillwater, over the hot concrete sidewalks that toasted my bare feet, up the hill to a shortcut through the ravine, up Mulberry Street, past the paved streets, to the gravel street that took me home.

Bud caught up to me just as I started toward the ravine, at the flat patch of ground where the Auger Brothers pitched their big tent when they used to bring their plays to town. He walked with me down into the sheltered, rocky depths of the ravine.

I always thought I would be tongue-tied if he ever talked to me, but in a couple of minutes, Bud had me feeling comfortable, even special, joking about me being barefoot and tanned like Tom Sawyer.

He put his arm around my shoulder, telling me that I had a "really great tan," then he patted me on the butt, joking about how damp my butt still was from the swim. At his suggestion, we were just ready to sit down and stretch out to dry off a little behind a big bush. The ravine was so cool and shaded, so private and so still, that we both jumped back when two little kids scooted out from behind a big boulder by the bush, screaming with glee at scaring us, and ran ahead of us up the trail.

We came on out, up to the sidewalk, back into the scorching sun, slightly disoriented from the heat and the interruption, and stood there a minute, blinking into the glare.

"I was going to see Bob, but I guess I better go back home," Bud said. "My mother wants me to run a couple of errands."

With this excuse, he gave me a playful cuff on the arm, swung around and started jauntily off, not back through the ravine, but taking the long way along Mulberry Street, whistling as he went.

I watched him go, forlorn and mystified.

When I saw him at Kirmser's those few years later, I was sure that he wouldn't recognize me, and if he did, he probably wouldn't speak to me, not in a queer bar. But he recognized me. He laughed in a surprised, delighted way and grinned— there was no doubt in the world that this was Bud York when he grinned—and he came straight over to our booth, his hand thrust out in greeting.

There was no subterfuge, no excuses, no pretense, nor was there any embarrassment on his part at being in a queer bar. He avoided any foolish remarks like, "My God, what are you doing here?"

Instead, he shook my hand eagerly, gripping it tightly, as natural and as easy as if we were meeting at Walgreen's drugstore after all these years.

"It's that good-looking kid from Stillwater," he exclaimed.

I wrenched myself out of the booth to stand up and shake his hand and he laughed at my confusion when I tried to introduce him to Lucky, Lou, and Ned, whom he did not know, and to Pete, whom he did know, having met Pete when he had been in Kirmser's before.

Bud York was completely in charge of the situation.

I was elated, overwhelmed and delighted that Bud York remembered me. He told me it was "swell" to see me again, making it sound like we had been old buddies, and he remarked how we always seemed to be running into each other at the beaches around Stillwater.

In the midst of my excitement and my astonishment at discovering him in Kirmser's, I suddenly froze. I was terrified that he would ask me what I had done and where I had been in the war. Pete was asking him if he hadn't been discharged yet, since he was wearing a uniform, and Bud explained that he'd put the uniform on for a reunion he had attended earlier.

I would have to lie to him about my brief navy time, because I was not about to admit to a wonderful guy like Bud York that I had been drummed out of the navy with an undesirable discharge. But my brain seemed frozen. I couldn't think of any kind of excuse. Lucky knew about my discharge. I had confided in him one night after we had gone to a movie and spent the night, or part of it, together in the Euclid Hotel. If Bud asked me, I would either have had to lie or admit the worst. I couldn't think of any other way to handle it.

I panicked for no reason. There was nothing to worry about, at least for now. Bud was enjoying talking about himself, recalling his football glories at Stillwater, the highlights of his military career, the friends he'd made in Germany, the volunteer work he was doing with boys at the same settlement house where Tony worked, his job, his girlfriends.

I was not surprised at his reference to girlfriends. It was part of the system, even at Kirmser's. And certainly if anyone would have girlfriends, it would be Bud York.

It seemed like magic that Bud York would show up in Kirmser's on a night that I was there. I sat in awed silence, afraid to move for fear of breaking the spell, glad that Pete was there to lighten things up. Pete, who always liked to act so nonchalant about things, was almost as impressed with Bud York as I was. When Bud asked me to go to a movie that Saturday night, Pete was even a little impressed with me.

He had dubbed Bud "The All-American Boy."

Even Lucky was proud of my friendship with Bud. Bud adopted a protective and patronizing attitude toward me, amused and affectionate, like an older brother. We went to the movies a couple of times and once Bud took me to the Gopher Grill, coming to my rescue when the bartender asked what I wanted to drink. I wasn't sure if it was the kind of place to order beer and the only drink I could think of was Coca-Cola. Bud ordered brandy and soda for both of us.

One rainy night, we went to see *Bataan* at the Paramount Theater, and afterward, Bud parked his car on a quiet street by Wilder Public Baths, on the hill just below Seven Corners. It was damp and even a little chilly as we sat there and talked. Suddenly, without warning, he leaned over and, gripping me by the shoulders, he kissed me, hard, straight on the mouth.

I had dreamed about this moment, fantasized about it, but it came and went and nothing happened. There were no sunbursts, no pealing of bells, no heavenly choirs. I didn't even get a hard-on. I sat there, chilled and dismayed at my lack of reaction, aware now that my feet were cold and feeling no more emotion than if I had just pressed my face into a damp, brick wall.

Bud must have sensed my dismay, my disappointment, my lack of response, because he settled back into the driver's seat, not saying a word, adjusted his hat, which had been knocked to one side when he pushed his face into mine, and we drove off in silence.

I had missed my last bus back to Stillwater, so Bud drove me down to the Levee, to Aunt Mary's, and I had to wake her up to let me in.

"Why didn't you call?" Aunt Mary demanded. "Can't you remember the number? Cedar 0980, is that so hard to remember? If I knew you were coming I could have got some doughnuts for breakfast."

I could hardly believe that nothing had happened. I was anxious, eager, even frantic to try it again, hoping that something would click, praying that the magic would happen. But we never went out alone again. Bud reverted to his big brother role the few times he came into Kirmser's after that.

As I thought it over, I wondered if that cold embrace, that peculiar reunion, was as much a disappointment for Bud as it was for me. I was almost nineteen years old now, and I had the odd feeling that Bud was still expecting an eleven-year-old boy.

Tony kept us posted on Bud's activities after he stopped coming into Kirmser's. He still showed up at the settlement house where Tony worked, she told us, befriending some of the boys. He had even offered to take Tony out some time if she'd wear a dress.

Tony was a handsome, Italian girl, as friendly and natural as a puppy, until she got up and swaggered about, in a grotesque masculine imitation, stiff-shouldered and self-conscious, as if her torso had been cast in concrete. A date would have been a good front for both of them.

But Tony was flabbergasted at the proposal. She wouldn't mind going out with a friend, even pretending it was a real date, but why should she put on a dress? She never, she said, wore dresses except to church.

"He's kinda stuck on hisself, ain't he?" She remarked when she told us of the peculiar terms of the offer.

She told us Bud York had become a Boy Scout leader, but still spent time at the settlement house, where the kids were dazzled by the flashy Oldsmobile he was driving.

Tony hadn't paid much attention to Bud and the boys he befriended until Bud took a special shine to a little Italian boy whose family Tony knew from the Levee. Bud took the boy camping, on picnics, to ball games. She talked to Lou and me about it one night.

"Youse guys don't think he's foolin around with those boys, do ya?"

Out of some misguided loyalty, I hastened to reassure Tony that I didn't think so, but even as I spoke, I remembered Bud's walk with me through the ravine that sunny afternoon a few years ago.

Lou seemed aware of the doubt in my endorsement and he told Tony: "Tell the kids they can talk to you if they've got any problems."

Poor Tony. She felt so guilty about her suspicions, and she was so impressed when we read later that Bud York had gotten married. A society wedding. He'd married a judge's daughter.

Lou was also very impressed. "How clever," he remarked.

I didn't say anything, but I knew what he meant.

5

The Girls

*I*LIKED TONY. I liked all the women who frequented Kirm-ser's. We didn't like to call them lesbians; that sounded too clinical. Sometimes we called them dykes, a strange nickname whose origins we never knew, but at least it sounded nicer than lesbians. They were a good bunch of girls, wholesome, honest, down-to-earth, full of comradeship and good humor, never as bitchy as some of the men. Ruth and Helen. Flo and Miriam. Barb and Donna. All of the girls in Kirmser's were paired off, except for Tony. All of them were young, too.

A couple of them were pretty dumb. Lucky, for instance, sometimes referred to Helen as "Dumb Dora." Helen was a tall, big-faced, sluggish blond who worked in a dime store. Her partner was Ruth, a packer at Montgomery Ward, a job she had landed when Ward's ran big ads offering women and girls jobs as packers at sixty cents an hour. Ruth was delighted to finally be getting a job as good as a man.

Helen and Ruth occasionally showed up at Kirmser's on Saturday nights. Helen was the femme and Ruth the butch in their relationship. Ruth was short, stocky, and very deft in her movements. She always dressed like a man—dark sweaters, slacks, a warm-up jacket or overcoat, plain brown oxfords, even a man's pocket railroad watch. She was always cheerful, even deferential in her treatment of people. Helen always wore skirts and blouses or skirts and sweaters. She wore makeup and dime store perfume. She had beautiful, shoulder-length blond hair, clean looking and soft. Her nose was her worst feature. It was long and very fleshy at the tip, with wide nostrils "like an animal's," Betty Boop had once declared. Helen's height was no problem for her. She carried herself well, with a slow, straightforward gait, unhurried and unperceptive, like a sleepwalker. She was a head taller than Ruth but that didn't seem to bother Ruth at all. Ruth acted like she had a goddess.

Because Helen was Ruth's girl, and because we all liked Ruth a lot, we always tried to be nice to Helen. If Helen came in early to meet Ruth and Ruth wasn't there—both of them lived at home—we talked to Helen, kidded around with her, made jokes.

Lucky and Dale would even stop in at the dime store to say hello to her when they were downtown on Saturday. She liked that, having good-looking men come by to see her at work.

"Makes me look like I'm popular," she told us.

One night while we were sitting with Helen, waiting for Ruth to show up, we started talking about Ruth, how nice she was.

"She's really a swell gal," Lucky said.

"We get along real good," Helen replied, and then, for some reason, as if to explain something puzzling, as if to clarify some obscure fate, she added wistfully, "She thinks I'm beautiful."

I marveled at the wondrous meaning of that remark. She knew she was not a pretty girl, but as long as she had Ruth she would be beautiful.

One day soon after this conversation, I saw Ruth downtown in the Emporium. I didn't recognize her at first. She was standing by the main floor escalator and, as I came up to say hello, I realized that she was with the older woman standing beside her. It was her mother. She had brought Ruth downtown shopping.

After Ruth introduced us, we stood there for a few minutes talking. It was hard for me to concentrate on what the mother

was saying, because I was trying not to stare at Ruth. Her cheerful, unassuming confidence was gone. She stood there, stricken,
our stocky little packer from Kirmser's, in a pink dress with a
lot of buttons on it, in ladies' shoes and nylon stockings, her
face pink with embarrassment, her lips painted. She was almost
cowering, as if she were trying to draw in upon herself, to somehow conceal this awful exposure.

Her mother continued to chatter, looking me over specula-
tively. She had been almost predatory during the introduction,
overenthusiastic, gobbling me up with her eyes, obviously delighted that she and Ruth should meet a young man friend of
Ruth's when Ruth, for once, was all dressed up.

There Ruth stood, all in pink, shifting uneasily from one
foot to the other in those awkward-looking high heels, her
nylon stockings baggy around the knees. And she was carrying
a purse. A purse, dear God. She was clutching it desperately,
not by the strap but by the body of the purse itself, holding
that great ugly purse up against her side, like a shield. It was
a large, black, patent leather purse with a shiny brass closure.
Ruth had a pained smile on her face, and her head was bowed
in abject humiliation. As I stared at her, fascinated at the purse
pressed against her side, I realized that she was also wearing a
brassiere.

I wanted to leave, but I didn't know how to escape from the
mother. I wanted to send Ruth a message. I tried mentally to
communicate this message to her: *I will never tell anyone that
I saw you like this.*

I remember Tony telling me once of having to carry a purse
when she went with her family to a neighbor's wake. The rest of
the women in the family had talked Tony into getting dressed
up, wearing a skirt, a blouse, and flats.

Tony said that she went along with it because it was a wake
and she understood how the Italians felt about women being
properly dressed for occasions like that. She had even agreed

to wear a little hat, but she had put her foot down at the purse
and she and her mother had gotten into a terrible argument.

"I never carry a purse," she had protested.

Her mother and her aunts had all insisted. Who ever heard
of a woman going out without a purse? the aunts demanded.
This is one time you're going to carry a purse, her mother
declared.

Her mother had begun praying, out loud, clutching her
rosary to her breast, begging Good Saint Anne for intercession
when Tony finally threw in the towel, snatched up the empty
purse donated by her mother, tucked it under her arm and
went with them to the funeral home, where she promptly set
the purse aside on a table and forgot it when they left.

That caused a bigger fight when they got home.

"Don't you care what you're doing to us?" her mother
wailed.

They believed Tony had left the purse behind out of spite.
It was a new purse, too, one her mother had recently bought.
It still had the tissue paper inside.

Tony offered to call the funeral home and, if the purse was
still there, to go back and pick it up.

The women were indignant about this. Horrified.

"Are you crazy?" they hollered.

The funeral home people would look inside the purse for
identification and discover an empty purse. What kind of
woman would carry an empty purse?

They forbade her to call the funeral home. No woman in
their family was going to admit ownership of a purse that had
absolutely nothing in it. It was better to suffer the loss of a new
purse than to admit to such a scandal.

Now here was Ruth, the Butch, trapped with her purse,
dressed all in pink, feeling like a fraud, anxious and awkward,
her mother mistaking Ruth's discomfort as an indication that
Ruth might be feeling something girlish toward me.

Ruth was finally able to pry her mother away, and she slunk

off, her nylons bagging at the knees in little pockets of despair, her purse stashed high up in her armpit like a rifle.

My father met my mother when he was working on the levee for Northern States Power Company, after World War I. Their courtship was opposed not only by Grandpa Fiorito, but, even more formidably, by Aunt Mary, my mother's big sister.

My dad was no Rudolph Valentino, but he was good looking and he was a war hero, even if he wasn't Italian. He was not only not Italian, he was English and Scotch. He was Protestant. And it got worse. He was ten years older than my mother, Bertha, who was eighteen when my father first met her. My father was also a widower with three young children.

Aunt Mary was livid and loud with anger and suspicion at this Anglaisman who would take Bertha away to some small town twenty miles distant, into a Protestant house with strange children. But my father, Lindsay, could read and write, which impressed my Grandpa Joe, who believed that if you could read and write—if you read books—you could get rich in America. That belief and Bertha's tearful prayers finally weakened his resistance, but never silenced Aunt Mary.

My father resorted to the telephone to make clandestine dates with Bertha, since Grandpa and Grandma Fiorito never used the telephone. Aunt Mary had ordered the telephone installed as an American mark of distinction when she first went to work, a luxury that Grandma avoided because of her poor English, and one that Grandpa distrusted. He was proud of it, but kept his distance from something that had come into his home that he could not feed, love, dominate, or bluff.

Once, when my father called, Aunt Mary, whispering and pretending to be Bertha, made a date to meet him uptown at Seven Corners. It was a cold winter night, and my father stood there for an hour, shivering and swearing, dressed in his suitor's thin, black, patent leather shoes, a new hat, a topcoat, and fashionable gloves. His feet were cold, his fingers stiff, and he had to slap his ears to keep them from being frostbitten. He was chilled with worry and concern over what was keeping Bertha.

When the deception was discovered, my father infuriated Aunt Mary by treating it lightly.

"By God, Mary," he said, "I never knew you had such a good sense of humor."

Aunt Mary never forgave my father, though Grandpa Joe finally consented to the wedding and he did the only thing a good Italian father could do under the circumstances: he threw a big, fancy wedding for his daughter, with bridesmaids, a flower girl, a ring bearer, a satin wedding gown with beadwork and a veil, and a spaghetti supper for the whole Levee.

Their wedding day is preserved in a long, black and white foldout picture series kept in a drawer, under the blue box that held the good silverplate, in the dining room buffet. With all the formal poses of the bride, the bride and groom, the wedding party, the ring bearer, the flower girl, and the bridesmaids, there stands Aunt Mary, a dutiful but belligerent maid of honor, a big, handsome woman with a wreath of silk rosebuds in her hair, a modestly altered flapper's dress, approved by Father Pioletti, and satin slippers on those big, capable feet.

Tony, like most of us, still lived at home. She was from the Levee, the Italian settlement in St. Paul where my mother's family came from, and where Aunt Mary now lived alone. Tony's family and my mother's family were not friends, not even neighbors. Tony's family lived on one of the backstreets under the bluffs near the railroad tracks, while Grandpa Joe had built his house on the front street, overlooking the Mississippi River. It wasn't prime property, since trash was always dumped on the riverbank to be washed away by high water in the spring, but it was more respectable than the backstreet houses.

All the Italians went uptown to the Holy Redeemer Church, and we knew one another more from church than from the

Levee. The Levee consisted of small frame houses built flush with the sidewalk and tiny fenced-in yards. The rest of the neighborhood was defined by two taverns, Vanelli's Grocery, and an abandoned schoolhouse that was used as a neighborhood center on Saturday nights, when short cartoons featuring Betty Boop and Felix the Cat were shown.

The only direct connection that Tony and I had was that Tony's mother and my Aunt Mamie, who became a nun, had been classmates at Mechanic Arts High School. When Tony discovered my connection to the Levee, she was delighted.

"I knew you looked Italian," she said triumphantly.

"Half Italian," I corrected.

"Which half?" she hooted, immensely pleased with her joke.

Tony and I used to trade Italian stories, always careful not to get too personal or to divulge any family secrets, and it was through this trading that we discovered a connection other than her mother and my aunt attending Mechanic Arts High School. It was our mutual dislike of Father Pioletti, the old Italian priest who ran the Holy Redeemer Church and the whole Levee with aristocratic authority. Father Pioletti had been an officer in the Italian army—in the First World War when the Italians had been on our side—and he commanded both obedience and respect from the Italian Catholics in our neighborhood. Even Grandpa Joe, as drunk and rowdy as he would get on feast days and American holidays, never forgot that Father Pioletti was Christ's spokesman on earth, a force that could make foolish brides cry, send bad men to hell, and cast unbaptized babies forever into limbo.

When Father Pioletti came to Grandpa Joe's house during feast day celebrations, honoring the household by taking a glass of red wine or a honeycake, other guests jumped to anticipate anything he might need. They melted away as he moved, gracefully and swiftly, among them, sought his blessing and bowed their heads as he spoke to them in that magnificent voice, mellow, cultivated, mysterious, and exotic, with that polished

Italian accent. It was a voice so beautiful, so rare, so intensely masculine, that it could have been God's own voice.

"He's like a dictator," Tony said.

"Like Mussolini," I agreed, and we both laughed.

Italian Americans despised Mussolini. He had embarrassed us with his silly posturing and his alliance with Hitler. It was okay to make fun of him, so I told Tony my Mussolini story.

I was in Garfield grade school when Mussolini invaded Ethiopia. I heard people criticize the Italians because Mussolini had used mustard gas against those innocent natives. I hadn't felt any particular connection to all this until one day at recess when Howie Benson ran past me and called me "Mussolini!"

I knew this was an insult, so I pushed him down the bank and he ripped his knickers and had to go home. Nobody called me Mussolini after that. Later, we all heard the news stories about what the Ethiopians had done to the Italian prisoners they caught in the desert. They slashed open their bellies, poured burning hot sand into their entrails and left them, gutted, to bake in the desert sun. Everyone, it seemed, was capable of brutality during a war. Like my dad said, "War is the shits no matter how you slice it."

My mother, in collusion with Aunt Mamie, had taken me out of public school in the sixth grade and sent me to the Irish Catholic parochial school. I turned to my father—a man of no religion—to rescue me, but he explained that when he married Mother, he had promised to raise their children Catholic. It was Mother's decision.

In that Irish Catholic school, I was Ricardo, an isolated Italian—half Italian although I looked all Italian—from the North Hill, the wrong end of town. My family's church was the old wooden French church, St. Joseph's, named for a carpenter. St. Michael's, a massive stone monster dominating the South Hill, was the Irish church; it was named for an archangel. Worse yet, I was the teacher's pet, because Sister Teresa, my teacher, was a friend of my Aunt Mamie (now Sister Eliza-

beth Louise) from their postulant days. The whole school
knew it.

I was ostracized, a silent, deadly blackball because even
those wild Irish assholes dared not verbally or physically attack
me and risk the displeasure of the nuns. Instead, they shunned
me. I ate lunch alone. I walked to school alone. I was never
asked to play in their games. I cowered in a corner of the school
yard at recess, an outcast, praying for recess to come to an end
so I could slink back into the formal security of the classroom
where even untouchables had their place. Even during that
forced march to Mass each morning, I was alone. We could
not speak, of course, but there was contact among the others,
elbowing, a quick whisper, an exchange of smiles. No one
looked at me. On Valentine's Day at the Garfield school, I
always got valentines from every boy and girl in my class. At
St. Michael's, I got two valentines, neither from boys. I was
numb with mortification and confusion.

On Columbus Day that year, Sister Teresa asked me, as the
only Italian in the school, to recite a "cute" dialect poem she
had found about Columbus. She was immensely pleased to
have a real Italian—at least half an Italian—and a nephew of
her good friend to mark this great occasion and perhaps to ease
the tension she must have noticed between me and the rest
of the school. I was to perform in assembly, before the entire
school, an Italian student honoring a famous Italian explorer
in an all Irish school.

I memorized that long poem carefully, perfecting the broad
gestures and the silly accent that Sister Teresa had coached me
in, and on Columbus Day, I walked out onto that bare stage
and faced a sea of hostility, a sullen, resentful audience that sat
perfectly still, ready to pounce, waiting for the dago to make a
mistake.

Sister Teresa was in the wings, at the side of the stage,
nodding encouragement, ready to cue me if I forgot a line as

I launched into the recitation, looking squarely out into all that hatred.

"Chreestofer Colombo, he leev acrossa da sea. His poppa, he sella da peanut and banan' een Eetaly . . . "

I went through it carefully, speaking clearly in that awful dialect, facing an army of contempt, making the proper wooden gestures, rooted to the floor, conscious of an audience that made no sound, that never smiled. When I had finished—performed the piece perfectly—I stood there, center stage, in silence and horror, not knowing what to do until finally, they put their hands together and clapped.

I never told that particular story to Tony. We stayed with the bright side of being Italian, the big weddings with their platters of spaghetti and barrels of red wine, when even old women like Mrs. Donatelli and Mrs. Columbo, defying age and rheumatism, would dance the tarantella. We stayed with the good food and the strange food, the octopus spaghetti sauce on meatless days, the chicken cacciatore, huge dishpans full of soaking lupini beans, tiny yellow moons in the still water, the wonderful aroma of simmering sauce flavored with neckbones cooking gently in the old tan enameled kettle. We stayed with the somber candlelight beauty of Midnight Mass on Christmas Eve, the old church smelling of hot candle wax, incense, garlic, and sweet wine, the tiny vegetable gardens our grandmothers tended on the riverbank across the road from their homes, every scrap of God's land turned into endive, tomatoes, and red peppers.

We stayed with the incredible, ghostly High Bridge. It straddled the Levee like some monstrous black spider with skeletal, trembling black legs, spanning from bluff to bluff across the wide Mississippi River. On summer days we sometimes climbed the steps from the Levee, our access to the world above, panting and triumphant when we reached the top, breathless again at the spectacle as we gazed down at the miniature world below us. How orderly all those little houses looked, how perfect the gardens.

I was astonished when I first learned that Mother had had to climb to the top of the bridge—steps eight stories high—every day to go to school, the Jefferson grade school on the north end of the bridge, after the Levee school was closed. Up those zigzag open steps in the snow, the bitter wind, the rain and the cold, the children came and when they got to the top, they ran along that plank sidewalk until they reached the shelter of the land and the trees at the end of the bridge.

"Every day?" I asked, knowing how tired I had been climbing those steps in the summertime.

"Twice a day," Mother said. "We had to go home for lunch."

"Why didn't you take your lunch?"

"We weren't allowed to."

"You had to go home for lunch? Up and down those steps? Every day?" I was incredulous.

"Every day."

"Why didn't Grandpa Joe complain about it?"

"Grandpa Joe would never say anything to the teachers. He was afraid they would find out he couldn't read or write."

Climbing a thousand steps a day and they couldn't bring their lunch. And I had been complaining about walking a mile to school where we got a hot lunch.

The girls, as well as most of the guys, lived at home, although Flo and Miriam were saving up to buy some furniture and get their own apartment. Lulu Pulanski, of course, had moved into his boyfriend's apartment, and acted as if he had never lived in the old tenement on Aurora.

Miriam was the prettiest girl in the place, small, dark, graceful, quiet. Even her smile was on a delicate scale, like the Mona Lisa, and maybe for the same reason. Miriam had bad teeth, neat little teeth but riddled with decay. She found in Flo, as we all did, an openness, a wholesomeness, a kindness that Miriam, as pretty as she was, could never match.

Flo was our entertainment in Kirmser's. She had a very pleasant singing voice, and on nights when the place was not very busy, we could sometimes persuade her to sing. Her favorite songs were "I'll Get By (As Long as I Have You)" and "When You're Smilin'." She'd lean up against the end of a booth, facing Miriam, who sat modestly ensconced in one corner, and croon sentimental ballads with a clear, sweet voice, as pure as a flute. She was shy about performing, but never self-conscious, and she was almost gallant in expressing her love for Miriam. We sat perfectly still during these performances, anxious to believe. Dickie Grant would get tears in his eyes at these romantic serenades.

Flo and Miriam were very earnest about getting a place of their own. They had shopped Cardozo's and found a bedroom set that they liked and Miriam was embroidering dish towels, doilies, and pillowcases for her hope chest. Both of them worked. Miriam was an elevator operator in the First National Bank Building, a prestigious job because it was well known that the bank hired good-looking young women to run their elevators. Flo worked in the factory where she had been since the war. She also had a part-time job. They had money in the bank.

Everything was all set except for one thing. Flo called me aside in Kirmser's one night to discuss it. She led me to an empty booth in the back of the place, and as she asked me to sit down, I knew this was going to be a solemn occasion.

She had something "kind of personal" that she wanted to ask me. She was asking me because she and Mimi both thought a lot of me. They had found a place they could afford and were moving in next month. Things were going great for them. Their dreams were coming true. What she wanted to know now was, would I father a baby for her and Mimi?

It never occurred to either of us that the mother would be

anyone other than Miriam. Flo and I were talking man-to-man. She and Mimi had some money saved up, Flo said, so Mimi could stay home and take care of the baby while Flo worked her two jobs. It was nice to be in love, but they really wanted a family.

I wasn't sure how to refuse, and as I hesitated, I glanced distractedly out of the booth and saw Miriam leaning out of the booth that Flo had just left, watching our booth. Our eyes met and Miriam smiled, not her ordinary Mona Lisa smile; this was a big, roguish, what-the-hell-let's-try-it smile, bad teeth and all, that shocked me right down to my socks.

I thanked Flo. I told her I had a lot of respect for her and Miriam. I was fond of both of them, but I couldn't do it. I wouldn't feel right giving up a child of mine.

Well, Flo said, doing her best to be fair about it, she probably wouldn't want to give up a child of hers, either.

She stood up, held out her hand, and we shook hands, still friends. She went back up front to break the news to Miriam. They left shortly after that, making sure to wave goodbye to me, to show that there were no hard feelings.

None of the girls spent a lot of time in Kirmser's. They'd meet there, have a couple of drinks, sometimes play twenty-one with Mrs. Kirmser, and leave early. They did not like to be downtown too late at night by themselves. One night, three or four of us were sitting in a back booth when Barb and Donna lumbered back to say goodnight before spending the night at Barb's folks' house.

"You going already?" I asked.

"Got to get home," Barb replied cheerfully. "We're way behind on our pussy eating."

Betty Boop looked like he was going to gag. A couple of us tittered nervously. As Barb and Donna strode out of hearing, Betty Boop hissed, "vulgar bitch."

We were never comfortable with one another's perversions.

6

The Survivors

WE WEREN'T TOO COMFORTABLE with anybody else's perversions, either, particularly those of the steady little trio—two men and a woman—who stopped by on most Saturday nights. I never knew their names, but I did know that the woman was married to one of the men, and the other man was her husband's lover.

They were small, countrified people, shy, polite, unremarkable in appearance. They would sit there on Saturday nights, ensconced in one of those old wooden booths, smiling at anyone who even glanced their way. They always looked snug, content just to be there, sipping at their beers, rarely talking, barely making any sound save for an occasional crackle as they nibbled away at a bag of potato chips. Once in a while one of them would get up and skitter away to the toilet.

My friend Pete, happily perverting an old nursery rhyme, called them the Three Kind Mice. Even though we were used to seeing them there on Saturday nights, and although they never bothered any of us, their presence was always a little disconcerting, almost an affront, because they were not like the rest of us.

A *menage aw twah* Lulu Pulanski pronounced it, then grandly explained to us what the expression meant. It boggled our minds. Most of us were in one-to-one relationships of whatever kind for whatever brief period of time, but here was a husband and wife and the husband's boyfriend carrying on God-knows-what kind of perversions. We were naively offended at this flouting of conventions, this mockery of marriage, this awful ambiguity. Most of us were defined, even confined, by our sexuality, and these three seemed to move fluidly from one partner to the other. It confounded us. Marriage, we'd always been led to believe, was for two people only. What these three were doing was more scandalous than divorce. At least people had heard of divorce.

There had been a big scandal a few years earlier when the King of England gave up his throne to marry Wally Simpson, an American who had been divorced not just once, but twice. The big joke about her:

Question: Why is Wally Simpson such a good checkers player?

Answer: Because she jumped two men and got a king.

All of us kids thought it was a great joke—a grownup joke—but when I told it at home, my father cautioned me about making fun of divorced women because Aunt Bert had been divorced.

Aunt Bert? Of all people. Aunt Bert, the skeleton in the closet? Married to someone other than Uncle Chuck, my dad's brother? It fascinated me. Aunt Bert and the Duchess of Windsor. It must have been years ago, I realized, before I was born, because she and Uncle Chuck had been married as long as I could remember. Aunt Bert would still cuddle up to Uncle Chuck—in that cute way of hers—and giggle that they were still on their honeymoon. Uncle Chuck would blush with delight at these moments.

They had no children. Aunt Bert loved kids, but kids made her "nervous," she had confided half-apologetically once to Mother. As a result, we always had to be on our best behavior when they came visiting. These were great ceremonial occasions, when Bert and Chuck came for Sunday dinner, arriving from Minneapolis in their big, beautiful, shiny black Chevrolet, Aunt Bert elegantly dressed in basic black and pearls, Uncle Chuck helping her out of the car as if she were as fragile as glass.

Aunt Bert was all the glamour we ever saw on Sherburne Street. I thought she and Uncle Chuck were rich, and I was just as surprised to find out that Uncle Chuck was only a foreman for Northern States Power Company as I had been to find out that Aunt Bert had been divorced.

But these three country mice. This *menage aw twah*. Divorce paled beside the kind of shenanigans we imagined they were involved in. Good or bad, gay or straight, we *knew* who we were, what our place was in this world. Yet these three, who knew anything about them? In the same way that most heterosexual people seemed to hate us because we were queer, because they really didn't understand us and so were afraid of what they did not know, we were afraid of the Three Kind Mice. We didn't understand them, so we wouldn't trust them. And it was a shame, really, that we were as bigoted as anyone else, that our own bitter experiences hadn't taught us any better lessons in compassion.

We rarely spoke to them, except for Pete and Clem, who professed an odd tolerance for this kind of thing. There were waves and nods between them and us, but they never presumed contact beyond that and we were content to leave well enough alone.

This scandalous trio, neither strictly heterosexual nor homosexual, was more offensive to us than the incestuous relationship of the two funny uncles of Lulu Pulanski, bachelor brothers who lived together all their lives, for many years in a dingy apartment building on Aurora Street, sharing the place with their sister, Lulu's mother.

Lulu had tried to keep his funny uncles a secret, but St. Paul is a small town and this kind of gossip found its way into

Kirmser's. Mick Flaherty's married sister lived in the same building as the Pulanski family; in fact, she shared a hall toilet with the Pulanskis.

The old Pulanski brothers were described by their neighbors as "odd ducks," "funny," or "queer," queer in this case used in its most innocent connotation. The gossip at Kirmser's was that the two old uncles had brought Pulanski out when he was still in grade school.

Pulanski had come a long way from that apartment building. He worked for Schuneman's now, a fine, family-owned department store, and his partner, one of the older guys in Kirmser's, had a good job with the Great Northern Railroad. Lulu had moved into his partner's apartment and redecorated the whole place: flocked wallpaper, new drapes, an Empire couch, a silver tea service, and a set of six colored prints of military men hanging above the couch, the soldiers in antique costumes of shiny black boots, great plumed helmets, red jackets, their shoulders and cuffs thick with gold braid, and white pants, as snug as winter underwear, tight on their legs.

Lulu had also begun picking out his partner's clothes, favoring sweaters and sportcoats instead of the conservative suits his partner usually wore. They were both very stylish, something right out of *Esquire,* the gentlemen's magazine that Lulu sometimes carried into Kirmser's.

His partner was nice enough, but funny looking, his eyes and the bridge of his nose sunk together in the middle of his face, concave, as if he had been kicked by a horse. His odd looks were a perfect foil for Pulanski, who, we all had to admit, was the epitome of good looks, the popular "tall, dark, and handsome" type, like a model in an Arrow shirt ad.

"Yeah," Pete conceded, "but he walks like he's got a pickle up his ass."

Pulanski's elegant airs got him in trouble once when he tried to snub Betty Boop, who had spoken to him one day in Schuneman's. Pulanski was standing with a couple of other well-dressed men, either customers or store management, when Betty Boop walked past and said hello.

Pulanski had not replied, pretending that he hadn't seen Betty Boop, so Betty Boop doubled back, coming face to face with Pulanski and his associates. He stopped, put his hands on his hips, and in his best little Betty Boop voice simpered, "Lulu, how nice to see you, honey," and then swished regally off. We howled with glee when Betty Boop told us that story. Pulanski was piss elegant but he wasn't stupid. He never tried to snub Betty Boop again.

The older crowd at Kirmser's, men who had held the same jobs for years, included Pulanski's friend. His job with the Great Northern was enviable because it was the railroad, a place of security and prestige, an overpowering presence in the city, its depot as big and magnificent as the cathedral, and much busier. The rest of the older, steadily employed crowd consisted of Pete, who was a Linotype operator; Ned, Pete's partner, who was a window trimmer; John, the silent librarian; Lou, who had a good job with West Publishing; the Edstrom brothers, who owned a little coffee shop; and Flaming Youth, who worked as a house painter.

There also was Clem, the only celebrity we had. He didn't do what we called work; he painted all day, not houses like Flaming Youth, but landscapes and portraits. He held art classes one night a week in the old Newton Building and he restored old oil paintings for some of St. Paul's prominent families.

Clem was in his fifties. He had studied art in Paris, lived in Algiers and Mexico, and during the depression he had been a big wheel in the WPA Federal Arts Project. He was squat, gray, bald, big-bellied, and as focused and self-contained as a buddha. It was hard to imagine that he had once been almost handsome. Photos he'd shown me from his days in Algiers pictured a solid young man with strong, almost arrogant features and dark, thick, carefully combed black hair.

Algiers, Clem told us, was where he'd been trapped into a

sandwich party. He was screwing an English professor's wife when the husband slid into bed behind him and began corn-holing Clem.

"There's nothing in the etiquette books that tells you what to do in a situation like that," he airily philosophized.

Those were the kind of tales that left us bug-eyed with wonder and glee, enjoying our secondhand sophistication until Clem would irritate us by talking too long or by failing to appreciate our pale offerings. Then we muttered among ourselves about the old windbag, making fun of how old, fat, and homely he was.

It was easy to do this until you noticed his eyes. No matter how drunk he was, those eyes always seemed to be measuring possibilities, taking stock. They were an ugly green, those eyes, like a cat's eyes, calculating, steady, and concentrated, measuring the distance before it would strike.

We made fun of—were even a little embarrassed by—the way he dressed. Once, to our great disgust, he wore a piece of clothesline instead of a belt around his waist, and he often wore a dark blue beret, a rakish-looking, lint-covered accent to the old face. Some of us still wore hats or caps —I'd splurged on a beautiful gray wool porkpie hat that got blown away one day on Seven Corners—but the beret was astonishing. Nobody else in St. Paul wore a beret; it clearly marked Haupers as an artist.

Clem was exceptional in another way: he lived with a woman. No one else that we knew or had even heard of was actually living with a woman except, of course, for the Three Kind Mice. Clem lived downstairs in an old stucco duplex on Ramsey Hill with his partner of many years, Clara Mairs, another artist, occupying the upstairs studio. Both made their living as artists, and if they were Bohemian by St. Paul standards, at least they were working Bohemians.

If we were sometimes irritated and sometimes impressed by Haupers, we were always a little leery of him, careful of what we said because he never hesitated to let us know when we had said something stupid.

One night Mick Flaherty, during one of his drunken flights of fancy, was bragging about his new boyfriend, claiming that his boyfriend had an asshole like a "pink tea rose."

Haupers guffawed. He leaned back in the booth, his big belly shaking, those odd green eyes alert to the kill, and roared with laughter. "Tea rose?" he challenged. "Do you know what a tea rose looks like? It's a big, showy rose. If you're trying to say your friend has a lovely little asshole, try rosebud. Tea rose may sound petite but it ain't. It's BIG."

We all laughed, except Flaherty. Flaherty was so full of bullshit that it was good to see him get slapped down once in a while, although Haupers, as usual, had been a little heavy-handed in his delivery.

Flaherty liked to make fun of other people, but he couldn't take a joke himself. He and I had been sitting in a booth one night when Clem came up to us and asked, in a confidential tone, "Do you know how you can tell if somebody jacks off?"

"How?" I asked, wondering what might be giving me away.

"Hair starts to grow in the palm of your hand."

Instinctively, of course, Flaherty and I turned our palms up.

"Ah," Clem said to Flaherty, "I see you're left-handed."

About this time, Clem asked me to pose for his art class, overlooking Flaherty, who was better built than I was and who often bragged about his physique.

Flaherty spent a lot of time lifting weights, following a Charles Atlas correspondence course advertised in pulp magazines as making a real man out of any skinny kid, turning a sissy who gets sand kicked in his face into the king of the beach. Flaherty strutted around Kirmser's like some kind of show horse, and among ourselves, we ridiculed his solitary obsession for body building. Nobody in his right mind would spend all that time engaged in such monkey business.

We were a little reluctant to cross Flaherty because we

considered him dangerous, not because of his muscles, but because of his big mouth. He was not only dumb, he was vicious. He'd been part of a gang that beat up a little queer in back of the eastside bowling alley one night. He had joined the attack to avoid suspicion when two old high school buddies invited him to join the party. After kicking the shit out of the little guy, they all went back into the bowling alley to celebrate. The odd thing about all this is that Flaherty was the one who told us the story, and we weren't sure if he was bragging about it or ashamed of it.

Because of Flaherty's volatile moods, his unpredictability, I wasn't too pleased when Clem asked me—in front of Flaherty—to pose for his art class in the Newton Building. I protested that I was too skinny, but Clem waved that objection aside, announcing that I had "good definition." I needed the money, so I agreed. I invested in a jock strap, and picked up a few extra bucks posing in the nude for Clem's art classes, and later posing for him in his studio.

It was a big, cluttered, dirty room—not just dusty but dirty—full of light, which at least brightened up the dirt. His easel stood in the center of the room and paintings of all sizes and shapes were stacked around the walls: landscapes, lake scenes, male and female nudes, a few formal portraits. One framed, enormous scene of the Minnesota River, a large expanse of sky blues, fresh greens and great, rollicking white clouds, took up almost half of one wall.

Clem lived downstairs, with a common hall outside for access to Clara's upstairs studio. Once when I was there, Clara rapped on the door, calling out, "Haupers!" Clem skittered about like a guilty schoolboy. He grabbed a gallon jug of red wine from a table near where we were sitting, hid it behind him, wiped his mouth with the back of his hand, and hastily opened the door for the impatient Clara.

"Haupers, have you been drinking?" she demanded.

With the gallon jug of wine behind him, half-empty from

the afternoon's tippling, and with the cheap wine heavy on his breath, Haupers loudly denied any such shenanigans. Clara glanced at me, glared at Haupers, and then, without another word, in a silence that reproached us far more than anything she could have said, she stomped back upstairs.

Clem shut the door, put the jug of wine back on the table, and resumed our conversation without even mentioning the interruption. I hardly listened to anything he said. All this time, I'd thought of Haupers as almost kinglike in his appearances at Kirmser's, but here at home, with Clara clearly in charge, he was just a bad boy.

They had been together for many years and in many places before they returned to Clem's hometown of St. Paul. The slight scandal of the two of them "living in sin" only seemed to enhance their reputations as real artists.

The youngest customers in Kirmser's were Dickie Grant and me. I was eighteen when I first came into Kirmser's and Dickie Grant was two or three years older. He was a silly fart who had a hard time keeping even the worst of jobs. He was given to small fits of pretention and foolish flights of fancy, but his pretensions were so harmless and so obvious, and he always seemed so vulnerable, that we tried to overlook these little deceits. He was silly, but he was never bitchy like Betty Boop.

Dickie was tall, spare, and goggle-eyed. He wasn't bad looking. He had wavy brown hair, a big smile—what Pete called a shit-eating grin—and big, round, vacant blue eyes. He carried himself well, shoulders well back and chin up, but there was something so rigid, so artificial, so patently false in this military-like bearing that he seemed as hollow and sexless as a celluloid doll.

His affectations included a pretense of speaking French, and he would always order a "glass of vino" when he came into the bar. He obviously didn't speak French, and didn't have the sense to recognize that "vino" was the Italian, not the French, word for "wine." He was like a ghost, some frail apparition, popping up at inconvenient and awkward times, pale and lost, anxiously looking for a place to rest.

Lucky could carry on a conversation with Dickie, but I had little to say to him. It was Mrs. Kirmser, however, who was so interesting to watch when Dickie would order a glass of "vino."

He really irritated her. She would bring him the drink in a thick, short-stemmed wine glass, set the glass down with a curt "here's your vine" muttered in that leaden German accent heavy with disdain, collect her quarter, and march off. It was not Dickie's effeminate manners or his foolishness that she disliked. She simply did not care for those who could not pay their own way, and there were many nights when Dickie Grant did not have enough money for even that one cheap glass of wine.

Dickie was no trouble, and he was always unfailingly polite to Mrs. Kirmser, but he was not a good customer. Mrs. Kirmser never showed the least aversion to or even the slightest interest in her customers' sexual preferences, but she kept a pretty good tally of who had steady jobs. Dickie was not only often without money and between jobs, but he also really didn't like to drink. He'd toy with his wine glass for hours, fondling it, fingering the stem, sniffing the wine to judge its "bouquet" when he didn't know the difference between dog piss and Dago Red.

If there was some sort of an occasion, any hint of someone's birthday or a stroke of good luck, if someone was embarking on a new romance, or on those nights when Flo serenaded Miriam, Dickie loved to offer a "toast." It was the romantic thing to do, and nobody in the world wanted life to be romantic more than Dickie Grant.

It made no difference to him as he performed these formal little rituals that it always was the same cheap muscatel that Mrs. Kirmser always served. It was the only wine she had. That glass of muscatel was his passport to the shelter and companionship of Kirmser's. He'd come into the bar, hover around any occupied booths, saying hello to any acquaintances, and if he had the money, he'd buy his glass of wine. He was always eager to join a group or to share a booth. He hated to sit at the bar, he said, because it looked like he was trying to "pick up" people. This coy little confession startled me because, up to then, I had never thought of Dickie Grant in sexual terms. He was always just that sexless, celluloid doll.

Our invitation to sit with us, almost always offered by Lucky, was not always gracious because we knew that once he sat down, we'd have him for the rest of the night; no one ever picked him up and he was too timid, too romantic to approach anyone himself.

Every time I saw him at Kirmser's, except once during Winter Carnival when he wore a sweater and slacks, he was carefully dressed, neat if a little rundown at the heels, always attired as if for some special occasion, in suit, shirt, tie, and worn but well-shined shoes. It was always the same dark blue double-breasted suit, a little too roomy for him, looking like it might have belonged to a bigger brother. Whatever he was waiting for in his ceremonial blue—that knight in shining armor, some hero on horseback, or Jack Armstrong, the All-American Boy— nobody ever carried him off from Kirmser's.

He dreamed of traveling, going to Mexico or "Gay Paree." He never made it to Paris, but he did get to New York City once, taking the Greyhound bus. He was there only a few days when he ran out of money, couldn't find a job, had no place to stay, knew no one, hadn't eaten for two days, and sent frantic collect telegrams asking for money to a couple of his queer acquaintances in St. Paul. One of them was Lucky, who took pity on him and sent him return bus fare, the exact amount. Dickie Grant rode the bus for three days and two nights, sleeping most of the time, exhausted and frightened, with nothing to eat except a couple of Hershey bars that he stole at a Greyhound rest stop in Pennsylvania.

Dickie lived with his parents in an apartment on Portland Avenue. He never talked much about his personal life, and he rarely mentioned his family, except to talk glowingly once in a while about a younger brother, a high school athlete, a football player, who was obviously the darling of the family.

When he came back to St. Paul, after his New York fiasco, he got a job selling women's shoes at Field-Schlick, where my Aunt Mary had worked in the children's shoe department for many years. Dickie was pleased when he discovered this connection. He seemed to feel that working with my aunt established some kind of relationship with me. When I'd stop by the shoe department to see Aunt Mary, he would drift over from the women's shoe department to say hello. He made me feel guilty because he was always glad to see me and I didn't want to be bothered with him. I had to explain to Aunt Mary where I had met him. I told her it was during Winter Carnival in the Ryan Hotel bar, a place where you could meet almost anyone in the world during carnival.

However, I didn't have to worry too long about running into Dickie Grant when I stopped by Field-Schlick. Aunt Mary told me he had been fired because one of the store's society customers had complained to Mr. Seesel that Dickie made her feel "uncomfortable."

Several years later, when Kirmser's no longer existed, I was back in St. Paul on vacation from the newspaper job I had in Ohio, and I stopped to see Aunt Mary at home. She still lived in the same stucco house she had been born in. She'd had it moved uptown from the Levee to Toronto Street when the city leveled the old Italian settlement down by the river; the Italians there had been outraged when one urban renewal expert referred to their plain, peaceful community as a "slum." Like their school, their homes were sacrificed to make way for a beautiful riverfront drive. Aunt Mary took that whole house uptown with her, just as other people might bring a photograph album, a dining room set, or a favorite quilt.

She had never married, and outside of trying to run the whole family, her only hobby was keeping scrapbooks of newspaper clippings, wedding invitations, postcards, birth announcements, obituaries, bylined stories I'd sent her from papers I'd worked for in Alabama and Ohio, and items about our family, her customers at Field's, friends, people she worked with, and Italian politicians.

She was showing me one of these scrapbooks when I noticed a little story about Dickie Grant, a two-year-old story, just a scant paragraph in the St. Paul paper, reporting that Richard Grant, twenty-nine, of Portland Avenue had been stabbed to death in prison, where he had been serving a sentence for writing bad checks. Aunt Mary pointed to that clipping.

"You remember him, don't you? He worked with me."

"Yes," I replied, so stunned that I didn't trust myself to say anything else. I was afraid to speak. I could hardly breathe. I felt like I was going to explode, an odd, expanding pressure in my head, like some enormous revolving merry-go-round was taking over the space in my skull, spinning and expanding at an alarming rate, a blur of brilliant mirrors and blood-red ponies. I knew that as soon as that wild carousel spun out of control and broke loose, I would scream.

I had to get out of there, had to escape before Aunt Mary would wonder at the depth of my grief over this silly sissy. I made a clumsy excuse and left.

Outside, as soon as I was out of sight of Aunt Mary's house, I broke into a run. Teeth clenched, tears running down my face, I raced along the sidewalk, muttering, "You bastards, you bastards." People moved aside quickly as I charged ahead. I ran desperately, trying to outrun the sounds in my head, a horrible ringing in my ears, sometimes as sharp and piercing as a scream. I ran until I was out of breath, exhausted, soaked with sweat, the ringing in my ears now as dull and mechanical as a rusty bell. Then I walked the rest of the way downtown.

Dickie Grant in prison. What kind of sadistic son of a bitch would send that harmless, girlish soul to a state penitentiary? Dickie Grant in prison. Dear God, you might as well pull the wings off a butterfly. Maybe being put to death was the most merciful thing that ever happened to him.

I had to talk about it, to give Dickie Grant at least a few minutes of mourning, some attention to his death. I went into Walgreen's and called Haupers.

He seemed pleasantly surprised to hear that I was back in town, and he invited me over for a drink. I walked over to Ramsey Hill, up to his place, feeling some relief in knowing that I could talk to someone else who knew Dickie Grant, someone as guilty as I was at the way we had treated him.

Haupers's place was as dirty and cluttered as ever. He moved some magazines off a chair and I sat down. He had been working at his easel, and when he waddled off into the dingy kitchen to find me a glass for the wine—a clean glass, I hoped—I looked around at his paintings on the walls, the Minnesota landscapes, the fleshy women nudes, a very bad portrait of an old man.

I remembered how impressed I had been the first time I had come to his studio and saw the paintings and imagined they were in the style of Grant Wood. I knew now Haupers was not a good artist, but I admired the way he worked steadily at it, not only at the painting itself, but at his self-promotion. That familiar old beret, the artist's smock, even that damned rope he sometimes wore around his waist were all calculated to present himself as the artist, the Bohemian. He loved to shock the occasional interviewer with his outrageous opinions on art and artists—"Picasso? He's a cartoonist!"—but he was shrewd enough to never say anything that could offend the good citizens of St. Paul.

I studied the portrait of the old man, an atrocious painting with no more life to it than the Masonite it was painted on. Haupers had a gift for color and composition, but he could not draw well and the rendering of the old man was flat and heavy handed; there wasn't a spark of insight or interest in it. Like Clem himself, there was nothing subtle about his paintings.

Haupers handed me the glass, a little greasy to the touch, poured it full of red wine, then settled himself into his easy chair, lit his pipe, and stroked a mangy gray cat that had jumped into his lap. The old place had mice and the cat was a working cat. Haupers peered at me with those steady, grayish-green, oddly unpleasant cat's eyes and asked cheerfully, "What's new in the news business?"

He had not known that Dickie Grant had been sent to prison and he was not concerned when I told him that Dickie Grant was dead. Murdered.

"Another fairy bites the dust," he said jauntily, dismissing the whole of Dickie Grant's life as trivial and unimportant.

The flippant remark caught me off guard, chilled and startled me, and I sat there in silence, hating the old bastard. I felt such a rage against him that I was sure he would notice it or at least sense it, but he was impervious to my reactions, as unaware of my hostility toward him as he had been at my grief over Dickie Grant's murder. He thought my mention of Dickie Grant was just small talk, an item thrown into the conversational pot along with any other tidbits about the old Kirmser crowd.

He had launched into one of his long monologues. Years of heavy drinking may have rotted his liver, but it never impaired his memory or his mouth. He could talk for hours, in great detail, and with unflagging interest, about himself and his experiences, his winters with Clara in Puerto Vallarta, the hypocrisy of the Catholic church, the years he was in charge of the art exhibit at the Minnesota State Fair, the technology of Art Deco, perversions in Algiers, politics in St. Paul.

Clem, I recalled, had never cared for Dickie, and I remembered now that once he had described Dickie as "useless," a description that at the time had baffled me.

My anger at Clem took the edge off my shock at Dickie

Grant's murder and I sat there, in Clem's dingy studio, hating the old bastard, wrapped up snug in my hatred like a warm cocoon.

This was the real start of my coming of age, my first doubts about mankind.

Nothing in the world had ever prepared me for truths like that. I looked at Clem now, studied him, my anger settling into judgment, a cold appraisal, the detached assessment of one stranger on a train speculating about the life of a fellow passenger. I saw Haupers for what he was, not necessarily good or bad, but a survivor. Despite adversity, failure, old age, the booze, he was a survivor. He was one of those people who get to the lifeboats first, like Lulu Pulanski, Bud York, or Betty Boop. What in hell did these people ever have in common with a loser like Dickie Grant?

7

Lucky

*L*UCKY WAS SOMETHING right out of the *Wish Book,* the name we gave to the big Montgomery Ward mail-order catalog that our families got during the depression. "I wish I had that" or "I wish that was mine." That thick, glorious catalog— almost eight hundred pages and weighing at least five pounds— was a winter's entertainment when I was a boy.

We'd often sit around the kitchen table near the stove those cold winter nights and page through that enormous book. Its slick polished pages, finished in a fine brown tone the color of new pennies, was crammed with beautiful pictures of clothes, toys, furniture, kerosene stoves and coal stoves, diamonds and windmills, bicycles, summer horseshoes and winter horseshoes, and flowery linoleum rugs so richly patterned that the makers of the catalog showed them in rare, full color. There were pictures of console radios and mantel models, banjos and ukuleles, shotguns and bear traps, studio couches that turned into beds and real beds and books of every variety. One page, advertising *Sex Facts Plainly Told* across the page from *Tales of Tarzan,* had been cut out by our mother, but not before I'd seen a curious reference to something called Birth Control.

We reveled in all the things we couldn't afford, dreamed of our favorite things, a cowboy outfit with a clicker pistol and a fire engine–red Lone Eagle coaster wagon for me, a horsehide aviator's helmet with ear flaps and goggles for my brother, an electric train, an Orphan Annie wristwatch that Elizabeth liked, bathtubs and water closets in glowing, glorious white, like marble, rare works of art that all of us, even my Dad, admired; all the things that Mother yearned for, a matching mohair living room set, a console radio, and her greatest dream of all, an electric wringer washer.

Lucky could have stepped right out of the pages of that catalog. He was good stuff, presentable, reliable, and of good value. It was almost as if he came with a lifetime guarantee.

Lucky and I had paired up for good shortly after Bud York had come and gone. Lucky was twenty-nine years old, nice looking, kind, well liked by everyone in Kirmser's, thrifty, honest, and good to his mother. He was fresh out of the army and back at his old job in the warehouse. I was lucky to have him and I hung on for dear life.

I'd thought he was more or less a newcomer to Kirmser's because he seemed such a regular guy—like fellows I grew up with—so I was surprised to learn that he had been among the first customers when Kirmser's turned queer. He was a friend of the choir director from his church, the man credited with "discovering" Kirmser's when the director and a couple of his friends, including Lucky, used to stop downtown after choir rehearsal for a discreet beer at Kirmser's between streetcar transfers. Kirmser's was a perfect little hideaway, unattractive, quiet, the drabbest place on the block, a bar struggling to make ends meet so it didn't take too many people too long to take over the place.

The choir director, meanwhile, after bringing Lucky out one afternoon when they'd stayed behind after choir rehearsal to straighten things up, had gone on to bigger and better things in Duluth, leaving Kirmser's to Lucky and a couple other customers who were "in the know."

Over the years, Mrs. Kirmser had developed a code of operation, almost an Italian *omertà,* for dealing with this strange new clientele. She never used any names, first or last.

Her customers were careful, even in introductions, never to give out a last name. It was considered bad business to even mention anyone's last name. It was first names only, and you would never tell a stranger where you worked.

Mrs. Kirmser carried this code one step further. If she was asked a direct question, even by a regular customer, about another customer, like "Has Joe been in yet tonight?" she would invariably reply, "I didn't nodiss." She was a model of discretion. She didn't know names and she never "nodissed" anything.

Most of us appreciated this discretion, even though it was annoying at times. After Lucky and I began going together, if I asked her, "Has Lucky been in yet?" I'd get that bland, blank reply, "I didn't nodiss."

Lucky lived with his mother in a small, dull, gray, two-bedroom stucco bungalow. He had been born and raised in the house, leaving it to go into the army and returning to it after the war. *Maw*, as he called his mother, was a widow, a good-looker when she was young judging from the old photos she kept on her bedroom dresser and on top of the radio in the living room. Having been widowed for a few years, and grown plump in her widowhood, she had developed a small network of "girlfriends," available companions for forays to the movies, free band concerts, shopping excursions, and "bumming around." It was a small but comfortable world, made up of her girlfriends, Lucky, her church, and the telephone.

She always primped to go out, even with the girls, and she'd check herself in the long mirror that hung in the tiny hall between the two bedrooms, making sure she looked as good as she could. I wondered if she, like Dickie Grant, secretly dreamed of being carried off by some shining knight on a big, white horse.

"I'm no chicken, but I'm a damn fine bird," she once cackled in coy good humor, partly for my amusement, I suppose, as she stood in front of the mirror. She was rouged, powdered, and perfumed, done up in purple finery, and as round, soft, and obvious as a plum.

"Maw," Lucky assured her, "You look great."

One afternoon when I was there, she was getting dressed in her bedroom, one of her girlfriends with her, and her friend was telling her how lucky she was to still have a son at home, helping out.

"Yes, but Mama still buys the coal," Gertie announced in a peevish voice, loud enough for Lucky and me to hear in the kitchen.

Embarrassed at this unexpected criticism, I glanced at Lucky. He wasn't disturbed at all.

"I pay my share," he told me matter-of-factly.

I'm sure that when I stayed for supper, or spent the night and had breakfast, arrangements had been made for Lucky to pay extra for his guest. This was simply the way they managed. Money was something to be cared for and tended to, requiring a necessary vigilance, like brushing your teeth or trimming your toenails.

His mother always ordered her groceries by phone from the neighborhood grocer when I stayed for supper. The telephone, a tall, candlelike black presence, as mysterious and ugly as a primitive, one-armed voodoo doll, stood on a little corner table, as solemn as a shrine. The only other object allowed on the telephone stand was a cheap, cherished souvenir from the 1939 New York World's Fair, a small ball and attached elongated pyramid, symbolizing progress, that stood guard before the telephone like a votive candle.

The telephone was a bosom friend, an idol, a confidante—the best kind of confidante, having no memory—a guardian angel, faithful servant, a thing of wonder to Lucky's mother. It was the most magical of all modern conveniences, more remarkable than a gas stove, as quick as electricity, more friendly than the radio. The radio entertained; the telephone worked magic. She could gossip anytime with her girlfriends, talk long distance—when rates were low—with her sister in Iowa and her son and grandchildren in Mankato, order her coal and groceries from the dealers, call downtown to complain about her taxes, make human contact whenever she was snowed in or feeling blue.

The telephone had brought the doctor when Lucky had a bad ear infection, when the boys had scarlet fever, and the night her husband died. The telephone was also her master. When it rang, she galloped from whatever room she was in or, if sitting down, she lurched awkwardly, almost leaping out of her chair to answer the summons, anxious, expectant, and curious to find out what voice would materialize, what message was forthcoming.

I got along well with her. She liked me, Lucky said, because I was "good-looking and lively," a little too lively for Lucky, I guess, when I tried a couple of times to talk him into letting me cornhole him. I didn't pursue it too much because he might expect the same thing from me and I wasn't keen to have anyone poking around in my butt.

Only once did his mother give any indication that she thought something might be amiss in the relationship between Lucky and me. She had waited until Lucky took the trash out to the backyard incinerator one night after supper to ask me where Lucky and I had met. We didn't work together; we didn't go to the same church; we weren't neighbors; we weren't even close to the same age.

We had met at Matt Weber's, where a waitress we both knew had introduced us, I told her. It was a clumsy lie, but it was the story that Lucky and I had agreed on. I knew Lucky had already told her this, but she had waited until I was alone with her, drying the dishes, to ask me how we'd met. It bothered me, but I looked straight at her and lied. I could tell by her reaction that she didn't believe me, and I suppose she wondered why we would lie about anything so simple. She never brought up the subject again. I think she was content with things the way they were, and I presented no challenge to the system.

We spent several cozy evenings together with his mother, listening to the radio, drinking Cokes, playing Chinese checkers or hearts, her favorite card game. She loved slipping the queen of spades—old "Slippery Liz"—to Lucky or me and sometimes I'd make a bad play just to give her the pleasure.

His mother had met Pete and Ned and Red Larson, all of us bachelors. She liked to kid us about our girlfriends and we played right along with her. I talked about Meg as if she were my steady girl. Pete let on that he was engaged to a girl at work. Ned mentioned his ex-wife. At least that was true. Ned, of all people, the flighty guy, had been married. He had stayed on good terms with his ex-wife, called her twice a month, remembered her birthday, and took her each year to his store's Christmas parties.

We thought we were smart and discreet. We were even careful not to use affectionate names with one another in private because we could slip up in public. I never called Lucky anything but Lucky and he always called me Rick. It was obvious to Lucky's mother that he had no girlfriend. She would kid him about being so "fussy" that he'd never get a girl, but she didn't seem bothered by this fact.

We were quick to act the gentlemen, opening doors for the ladies, carrying their parcels, walking on the curbside when accompanying them on the street, giving up our seats on streetcars and buses. We made ribald and clumsy jokes about pinups like Betty Grable and Rita Hayworth whenever one of their new movies came out.

None of us followed sports except Pete, so we counted on him to bail us out of embarrassing spots if the subject ever came up with straight guys, or when Hazel, a friend of Lucky's mother, brought up the subject of baseball.

Hazel was a big fan of the Saints, which we thought was a strange hobby for an old lady. Most old ladies knit or crocheted, but she sat glued to the radio when baseball games were broadcast, and on Ladies Day, when women got in for thirty cents, she took the streetcar out to the ballpark.

She was like my Aunt Bert, another unlikely baseball fan. As elegant as she was, Aunt Bert sometimes went with Uncle Chuck to baseball games in Minneapolis. Appropriately attired in a nice summer print dress, she cheered the Millers, ate hot dogs, and even drank beer, just like a regular guy. Uncle Chuck adored her for being such a good sport.

The one risk we all took was going to Kirmser's. It was a close call for some of us. Aunt Mary worked only a block away, at Field's. Mick Flaherty's mother was a night waitress at Matt Weber's. The jewelry wholesaler that Mother Jerusalem's uncle did business with had his headquarters downtown. Any neighbor or relative shopping downtown might see us going into or coming out of Kirmser's.

One quiet night, in the middle of the week, one of the dangers of going to Kirmser's caught up with us. Our worst fear was realized. A fight broke out in Kirmser's, a disturbance that could bring the police or, worse, public exposure in the newspaper.

Lucky, Haupers, Ned, and I were sitting in a booth. Tony and Tom Clark were talking to one another at the far end of the bar, and Flaming Youth was sitting by himself in his usual place at the front end of the bar, reading the paper, his back to the door.

Two strangers came in, a couple of guys in their twenties, still in their work clothes—dungarees and jackets—and stood up front near Flaming Youth. We had all turned when the door opened, and we checked out the newcomers as they came in and crossed over to the bar. Then we went back to our conversation, dismissing them as nothing special, a couple of laborers who had accidentally wandered in.

Suddenly, one of the newcomers turned to Flaming Youth and asked loudly, "Are you a queer?"

We could hardly believe our ears.

Before he had a chance to say anything, one of the men hit Flaming Youth, knocking him off his stool. His newspaper flying apart, he sprawled on the floor, where both men kicked at him, rolling him up against the front wall. When he brought up his arms crisscrossed, elbows out, to protect his head, they kicked him in the stomach.

Flaming Youth kicked out his feet to try to ward them off, but one foot got caught behind the steam radiator on the front wall. He was on his side, facing them, awkwardly trying to wrench his foot loose from the radiator. As he twisted and turned, his arms held up to protect his head, the two men continued to kick him in the stomach.

Before I knew what I was doing, I was up, out of the booth, and up to the bar where I grabbed a beer bottle by the neck. Mrs. Kirmser was shouting, coming from behind the bar. I raised the bottle over the head of the stranger nearest me, but I hesitated, afraid that if I hit him too hard I might kill him. In that second of hesitation, his friend called out a warning, and the man turned and saw me poised with my bottle. He punched me in the jaw, knocking me flat on my ass on the floor. Then, just as suddenly as they'd come into the bar, the two men bolted. They ran out the door. No one tried to stop them.

Mrs. Kirmser and I helped get Flaming Youth's foot free from the radiator, and when he got to his feet, he picked his watch cap up from the floor, put it on, and straightened his jacket. Embarrassed by the whole incident, he quickly made for the door.

I stopped him until I had a chance to look outside to make sure the two men were gone. The coast was clear, and Flaming Youth limped out, never saying a word.

I felt foolish, trying to hit somebody with a beer bottle and getting knocked on my ass in the process. As I crossed back to the booth where I had been sitting, I saw Mick Flaherty and his new friend, Ramblin' Rose, with their heads poked out of the end booth.

I sat down beside Lucky again, feeling my jaw to see if it was broken. It was sore, but it was still working. No one said a word for a couple of minutes, not even Haupers. They looked at me as if I were a stranger, an unexpected and unsettling appraisal. Then Lucky finally spoke.

"Why did you get into it?" he demanded.

I was stricken silent by the question. Why? What did he mean, why did I get into it? I didn't know how to reply to such a stupid question. Were we all supposed to sit there while two guys kicked the shit out of an old man like Flaming Youth? Maybe I hadn't done too well, but at least I helped break it up. And where were the rest of them? Haupers was too old and too fat to fight. So was Mrs. Kirmser. Mr. Kirmser was too old and too slow and probably didn't give a shit. But what about Lucky, Tom, and Ned? What about Flaherty, the big muscle builder, the Charles Atlas of Kirmser's? He could at least have stood up and flexed his muscles, maybe kicked some sand in their faces. Ramblin' Rose could have screamed.

Tony had been at the bar, too, talking to Tom Clark, who had disappeared immediately after Flaming Youth left. Tony might consider herself butch, but was she supposed to single-handedly defend eight queers from a couple of bullies?

Could we call the cops? Not us. *We* were the criminals.

Flaming Youth was back in the bar the next week, talking to Lou. He was limping a little, but he looked okay. We waved at one another. We didn't speak. I hardly knew him. I'd never had a conversation with him in my life.

Even so, I discovered that he and I were the newest gossip item at Kirmser's. Lucky not only chastised me for getting mixed up in the fight, but later told me Clem's reaction to my getting into it. He phrased it like a question, almost an accusation.

"Clem thinks you must have an 'interest' in Flaming Youth to get mixed up in the fight like you did."

That was too much. Flaming Youth was old. He was bald.
He was the biggest whore in town. Christ, he had hair in his
ears. Lucky could be dumb at times but I was really surprised
by Clem's reaction—that the only reason you would help someone is if you had an ulterior motive, figured you might get
something out of it.

I couldn't believe these people. I didn't want to believe these
people if they couldn't understand anything as basic as helping
a friend in a fight, helping one of us against all of them. Whatever we thought of Joe, he was "one of the boys." He belonged
to the lodge.

Flaming Youth, or "Joe" as I came to call him when the
childish pretense of nicknames fell away, and I became friendly
after that. We didn't talk so much at Kirmser's, since Joe seemed
aware of the gossip there and was concerned that it might em-
barrass me; we met and talked around town. We'd usually see
each other on Saturday afternoons after I got out of work. Joe
was always around town.

It was awkward the first time we actually stopped to talk to
one another.

"Where you headed?" I'd asked, a dumb question and none
of my business.

"I'm between toilets," Joe replied cheerfully, breaking the
ice. We both laughed.

Neither of us mentioned the fight. Even after that, when
we began having coffee together and I got to know him, better
than most people in Kirmser's knew him, we still never mentioned the fight.

Joe never condemned anyone for not helping him that night,
but he never forgot that I was the one who had. He was han-
dling it better than I was. I was angry at Lucky, surprised, disgusted. Worse than that, I'd come to the cold realization that
this small brotherhood of mine was no better than some of the
bastards outside.

Lucky and I were not exactly meeting the standards we'd

expected of one another, but we were hanging in there. He was the best security I had. Yet it still rankled me that he had refused to help Joe, and it made me even angrier that he was angry and suspicious that I had.

I never said anything to Lucky, but I was not good at concealing my feelings and I'm sure he knew how I felt.

My defense of Joe had created a whole new atmosphere in Kirmser's, even affecting Mrs. Kirmser. She looked at me now, I mean, she really looked at me, like a friend or a neighbor; she smiled at me and there were a couple of times I would have sworn she was going to call me by my name.

About this time, Lucky chose to express disappointment about my teeth. He was extraordinarily proud of my smile. He bragged about my smile, gloated over it. A perfect smile. Nice white teeth.

One night I mentioned a problem I was having with a filling. Lucky looked shocked.

"You told me you had perfect teeth," he charged.

"No, I've got two fillings."

"You never told me that."

"They're in my back teeth," I said, trying to reassure him.

His disappointment was enormous, and out of proportion to the reality of the situation. He decided to see it all on a more dire and symbolic level; what he thought was perfect was flawed. He had been bragging about me over something that wasn't right. He felt I had let him down.

We still had our good times, despite these small disappointments, like the time he took me to a drag wedding in Excelsior, out around Lake Minnetonka, way on the other side of Minneapolis.

It was at the home of a fellow that Lucky had met in the army. The host gave us detailed instructions on how to get there, and we left early in case we got lost. Neither of us had spent much time in Minneapolis, and none at all in a place like

Lake Minnetonka. If Minneapolis was foreign, Lake Minnetonka was another universe.

Lucky's friend kept trying to keep the wedding party in the
cottage, but some of the guests insisted on spilling out onto
the lawn. One, dressed up like a Bette Davis bridesmaid, an
ugly little guy in a shiny, pink formal with puffed sleeves and
a sweetheart neckline, was wild. He wore a silver cloche and
his hair was combed forward in bangs. I had never seen anything like him.

"Petah!" he kept screaming at people, mimicking a greeting
Bette Davis had used so effectively in one of her movies. "Petah!"
he screamed out over the lake as he ran down to the shore,
clutching his breast and scanning the horizon as if searching
for a lost ship.

He stood dramatically on the beach, a pink figure of great
tragedy, until his exasperated host finally coaxed him back inside. He kept smoking cigarettes, making jerky movements
with his arm and spitting out little clouds of smoke, just like
Bette Davis. There were brown stains on the fingers of one of
the long, white gloves he was wearing. Sometimes he tucked
his bouquet of red roses under one armpit while he lit up another cigarette.

The bride and groom, perfect little wedding cake figures,
were cute, the bride in an enormous white dress and veil
crowned with seed pearls, and the groom in a formal cutaway.
Yet they and the two other bridesmaids were upstaged all afternoon by Bette Davis, who came down the aisle with one hand
on his hip, twitching his hips and shoulders, and rolling his
eyes. He stopped in midaisle and announced that due to the
seriousness of the occasion he would not smoke during the
actual ceremony. We shrieked with laughter.

The fellow who acted as the minister, in borrowed white
collar and black suit, listed an uncle who was a priest as his
reflected credentials to perform the ceremony.

There was champagne, a white, three-tiered wedding cake

with pink roses, and little silver dishes filled with pastel-colored mints and mixed nuts.

The guests all kissed the bride and groom, and in all the commotion, the screaming, the hugging, the laughter, the loud music on the record player, only the groom looked subdued. He looked wistful, even rather tragic, anxious for his bride and bravely determined to make the best of things.

I was unsure about the whole performance, sympathizing with the dilemma of the groom and slightly shocked at this sacrilege of a wedding although I laughed as hard as everyone else. I made the mistake of mentioning my doubts when I was talking to a slim, good-looking blond from Minneapolis, who dismissed my provincialism with an arch, "Well, of course, you're from St. Paul."

Lucky was also irritated with me when I tried to explain my feelings on the way home.

"Why do you want to make a big thing out of it?" he demanded. "I thought it was kicky."

The glow was obviously off our romance. I had seen a side of Lucky that had shocked and angered me, and he, in turn, had discovered a flaw in my character; I was a liar with imperfect teeth. Yet we still felt a commitment to one another, we were a couple, we were partners, lovebirds, as Dickie Grant would say. We were one of the steady couples in Kirmser's. We were glued together by what other people expected. And, of course, we still had sex, carefully and without conversation in that little bedroom across the hall from his mother's room.

We continued to make our occasional excursions on Sundays across the St. Croix River to Hudson, Wisconsin. We'd take Lucky's old Chevy—Pete and Ned, Lucky and me—and head for the Badger Lounge, one of Pete's favorite spots.

Kirmser's was closed on Sunday because of Minnesota's blue laws, but Wisconsin was wide open, a state chock full of beer joints, honky-tonks, and roadhouses. Anyone who wanted a little action on Sunday headed for Wisconsin. The Wisconsin hosts were cordial and sympathetic to Minnesota visitors, and Pete buddied right up to them. It was a harmless conspiracy, a feeling that we were putting one over on all those hard-nosed Puritans, the Prohibitionists, the Blue Noses who stopped us from drinking on one side of the river, but who couldn't touch us on the other side. The only time I ever missed Sunday dinners at home was when we made those trips to Wisconsin.

I enjoyed Sunday dinners at home. The whole family got together at our house, gathered around the dining room table— the kids in the kitchen—crowded together on mismatched chairs, the late afternoon sun shining on the assorted china, turning ordinary water glasses into sparkling goblets, and warming the good silver plate, a wedding present from Aunt Mary. We were better off since the war; my father was working at the post office, and Mother was selling shoes afternoons at Janda's. Mother sat at the head of the table, her face flushed from the heat of the kitchen, pleased at being able to offer a plentiful table. Her home now had a bathroom and her husband was working full time. Some of her prayers had been answered.

On the occasions when Aunt Bert and Uncle Chuck would drop in from Minneapolis at dinnertime ("Just to see you kids—we had dinner at the Grand Café"), chairs were pushed even closer together and they would graciously allow themselves to be talked into having dessert. Their appearance always transformed the dining room from its usual mild uproar into a festive occasion, their arrival reminding me of Father Pioletti's descent into the dining rooms of the Levee.

We feasted on pot roast or roast pork and mashed potatoes or chicken and dumplings, always topping it off with my dad's famous homemade pies. Mother cooked; Dad baked for the Sunday gatherings. He had learned to cook as a boy in the lumber camps, before he and Uncle Chuck had enlisted in the marines, and his lemon meringue, pumpkin, and banana cream pies were delicious, the baked meringue in golden brown peaks, the crust light and flaky. It was a marvel to me how he could turn anything as slimy as lard and as dull as flour into such tender crusts, bringing the greatest praise from Aunt Bert.

"Lindsay," she would coo, "you've got the magic touch." We basked in her compliments because, as she often gaily reminded us, she was French and the French were experts on fashion and fine cooking.

I was willing to miss some of those pleasant Sunday get-togethers with my family to escape once in a while, with Lucky and my queer friends, into the welcoming beer joints of Wisconsin. Even after my relationship with Lucky ended, those Sunday trips, playing hooky from my usual life, remained among my fondest memories.

8

The Guy with Crabs and Other Visitors

*V*ISITORS STOPPED IN KIRMSER'S once in a while, sometimes long enough for us to recognize them, sometimes long enough for us to get to know a first name or identify some personal peculiarity. For instance, the Guy with Crabs. We also had occasional strangers, especially during Winter Carnival, men who made discreet connections, then disappeared forever. We were suspicious of these one-night stands, unknown men who left behind nothing more tangible than memories.

Still, we liked some of these irregulars, like Louie, the theater student from the University of Minnesota in Minneapolis, and Tom Clark, a business major there. Both were going to college under the GI Bill, which provided college educations for veterans with honorable discharges, and both were building good futures for themselves. Before the war, only rich kids went to college, and only rich kids were expected to go to college. Now regular guys like Louie and Tom were getting a break. We felt a proprietary interest in their education because their successes felt like our own, and they reminded us that new opportunities, new directions, were possible.

Harrison, my best friend from high school, my soulmate there, was one of the brightest kids in our class, and like me, he was one of the poorest. Yet, he was going to college, and he had actually been accepted at Harvard after the army. Harvard!

Holy Moses. Ivy League—whatever that meant. Out East. Going to college was a dream in itself, but who would ever imagine going to such an exclusive place as Harvard? Who would believe Harvard would take him? How did he even think about it? The day Harrison told me, I could hardly wait to get to Kirmser's with this news. My best friend was going to Harvard. It felt like something I should brag about.

"Harvard?" Haupers said flatly when I told him. He was clearly abashed at the news. "Well, you can kiss that friendship goodbye."

What a shitty thing to say. I couldn't fathom his reaction. What kind of a friend did he think Harrison was? We'd been friends since kindergarten. We knew the worst secrets about one another. We were soulmates. Did he think Harrison would drop me just because he was going to Harvard?

Louie, on the other hand, overwhelmed with his own good fortune at being able to go to college, was impressed with Harrison's spectacular achievement.

"Wow!" he said, and he meant it.

Louie, whose future, when he was in high school, appeared to be an endless job on the production line at Hamm's Brewery alongside his father, was dazzled at finding himself not only in college, but in that part of college he referred to lovingly as the "*theatuh!*" He pronounced the word broadly, grandly, his tongue snapping against the back of his front teeth like a whip as he spit out the *tuh!*

When he'd take a break from his studies and drop in at Kirmser's, Louie brought the theater with him. After a couple of beers, without the least encouragement, he'd sometimes launch into Hamlet's soliloquy, Iago's treachery, or Lady Macbeth's troubles with those damned spots.

"Drunk on Shakespeare," Pete once remarked.

Louie wasn't just drunk on Shakespeare; he was intoxicated with the joy of learning, delighted to have the opportunity, and committed to making the most of his good fortune. He never

Ricardo with his parents,
Bertha and Lindsay Brown.

Ricardo, nearly two years
old in 1928.

With grandmother
Archangela Fiorito
and baby sister
Elizabeth in 1931.

At age five.

Ricardo (right) and
half-brother Norrad.

Ricardo and Elizabeth
with their mother in
1934.

Ricardo and Norrad, 1938.

At home in Stillwater with Elizabeth, brother Robert, and Bertha, 1945.

Boot camp, U.S. Naval Training Station, Great Lakes, Illinois, December 1944.

Family portrait, 1945.

Court reporter and sports
editor for the *Fairbanks
Daily News–Miner,* 1957.

Book jacket photo for *Cold Beer,* published in 1972.

Relaxing with sister Elizabeth, 1987.

Hard at work on the
manuscript, 1994.

just studied; he made a game, a sport, almost a religion out of learning.

One night he came into Kirmser's and told us he and some of his friends had had a Browning festival the night before.

"You had a what?" Pete asked incredulously.

"A Browning festival," Louie repeated. "We're studying Elizabeth Barrett and Robert Browning. You know, the poets?"

Pete and Haupers roared with laughter.

"Good God," Pete said, "Somebody tell him what browning means before he makes an ass out of himself."

"And gets browned," Haupers gleefully added.

Poor Louie. He was a good sport about it. Even a college kid could learn something from the old-timers in Kirmser's.

There was another college student who sometimes visited Kirmser's, but he wasn't on the GI Bill. Angus had been studying for the priesthood, but had returned to his family home on Grand Avenue to reconsider his decision. He was tall, awkward, and obnoxious, both clever and ugly in a cold, supercilious way. He and Clem got into a long, ongoing argument about Roman Catholicism.

Clem surprised me with the vigor with which he attacked the church. He and I were both lapsed Catholics, but while I was content to leave and forget the church—an organization I considered sinful in its condemnation of other religions— Clem had left it only to become obsessed with it. Clem considered the church a fraud, an exploiter of the poor, a power both proud and perverted.

The winter Angus first appeared, whenever he got bored with bridge parties, cocktails at the Commodore, or engaging in bonspiels at the Curling Club, he showed up at Kirmser's, and if Haupers was there, they would get into it. They argued about the Inquisition, the morals of the popes, celibacy, whether Christ was a queer and, if so, what he liked to do in bed. They argued about the Virgin Birth, the selling of indulgences, the riches of the Vatican, the politics of Archbishop John

Ireland. It was great entertainment for Angus, who loved to argue, and a real challenge to Clem, who took his dislike of the church very seriously. The only thing that could drown the two of them out was Louie launching into an impassioned rendition of Lady Macbeth's famous hand-washing monologue.

After a few weeks of arguing with Clem, Angus found a new diversion. He brought him into Kirmser's one night to show him off—an eighteen-year-old blond, bashful Swedish Lutheran, a real beauty, whom Angus was trying to convert to Catholicism. He had plucked the guy out of the gas station where the young man worked and taken him under his wing, stoutly denying any sexual hanky-panky in the relationship. The Swede was obviously impressed with Angus's affluence, intelligence, and authority, assets about which Angus never bothered to be the least bit modest. Angus worked on the Swede for weeks, preparing him for the conversion, taking him to dinner, to church, to concerts, to the theater, and one weekend, just before Angus planned to return to school, to Chicago.

After the Chicago trip, Angus couldn't wait to tell us the outcome. Blithely disregarding all his previous declarations regarding the nonsexual nature of their relationship, Angus announced that he had finally "had" the young man. It wasn't a confession; it was an ebullient, proud recounting of a glorious one-night stand. They'd taken the "400" to Chicago, the first train ride the young Swede had ever been on. In Chicago, after dinner, drinks, and a movie, they had returned to their hotel room and were cleaning up before going to bed. When the Swede stepped out of the shower, Angus brought him another towel, offering to dry him off, and after rubbing his back, Angus spun the Swede around, fell to his knees and took the kid's cock into his mouth, reverently, like Holy Communion.

Clem was outraged at this hypocrisy. He spluttered with indignation when he heard the story, but Angus was blasé, even smug, about the whole episode. He was mildly amused at Haupers's reaction, pointing out that this one encounter was completely incidental to the kid's conversion. For weeks, after Angus had gone back to school and the Swede had actually entered a Catholic seminary, if anyone mentioned Angus or the young man, Haupers's eyes would bulge, his jowls tremble, and he'd bellow with outrage at this case of a person who, he said, was "literally sucked into the church."

The Guy with Crabs was a forlorn, young fellow who never had a chance to score because the Kirmser gossips warned everybody who got near him that he had crabs. I saw him in Kirmser's three or four times, a shy, bewildered outcast, always alone. He was rather appealing, sweet almost, in his melancholy solitude. He wasn't bad looking, but he was always on the scruffy side, with a constant five o'clock shadow that, meek as he was, made him look faintly sinister.

I began asking people if they knew anyone the guy had infected. No one did, at least no one admitted it, although I had my suspicions about Pete. He was rabid about the guy.

"How does anyone know the man still has crabs?" I asked. They just knew.

"He doesn't scratch much," I protested, watching the guy standing there, snubbed, ignored, bewildered, trying to look casual, like me at recess in St. Michael's Catholic School.

"He's had them so long he's used to them," Pete snapped. "That's why he doesn't scratch anymore."

There was no hope for this guy. He was a marked man.

The night Bart first brought his new friend Wayne into Kirmser's, it was one of those ugly Minnesota winter nights, the temperature a few degrees below zero, streets almost deserted, the sky a dirty gray. There was a light cover of snow on the ground, a chill wind pushing the flakes about in gusts and swirls.

Wayne, when he shook hands with all of us, exposed a fringe of the always unavoidable winter underwear under his sleeve.

Pete hooted at that. "Farmer's underwear," he teased.

"It's cold out," Wayne replied, moving close to Bart and glaring at Pete in instant dislike.

It was an awkward situation and Lucky tried to smooth things over.

"Don't get worked up, Wayne," he counseled. "Pete's just kidding."

But Wayne did get worked up, angry at this unexpected insult from a stranger, and he sailed grandly out the door, dragging an unhappy and red-faced Bart behind. Wayne refused to come back into Kirmser's after that, huffily telling Bart that he never expected to be insulted in Kirmser's, of all places.

Bart was one of our occasional visitors. He strayed in once in a while after his night shift as a punch press operator, a trade that left him with one digit missing, down to the knuckle, on the middle finger of his left hand. He was well-liked and a particular favorite of the girls, who apparently found in him some of the same good nature and wholesomeness that they possessed.

Bart was crestfallen at the way things had turned out, so Lucky suggested that if Wayne wouldn't come into Kirmser's, maybe we could double-date with them sometime; we could go to a movie or get something to eat at Matt Weber's or some ice cream at Bridgeman's. Bridgeman's was a special place at that time; it sold only ice cream, nothing fried or cooked, so it always smelled clean and fresh. It was a cheerful place, brightly lit, with huge, plate glass windows.

Wayne did agree to the double date, but coax as we would, he always refused to come back to Kirmser's. His indignation was renewed each time we mentioned the place. He would never, he insisted, forget being insulted by his own people.

Only one black man ever came into Kirmser's, and none of us liked him.

I had only seen African Americans—we called them Negroes

then—in the navy, at a distance, and I had spoken to only one black person in my life.

When I was editor of our high school paper, some of us took the bus from Stillwater to Minneapolis to see a stage show and a movie at the Orpheum. The stage show featured Peg Leg Bates, an old, black, one-legged tap dancer. I interviewed him backstage after his performance, and wrote a story about him for the school paper, extravagantly praising his courage, his talent, and the inspiration that he provided all people, particularly black people and, of course, one-legged dancers.

The only black men I had seen in the navy were in the reception area when I first arrived at the Great Lakes Induction Center. All of the white recruits watched them, fascinated, from across a big, chilly room, where they had been segregated into a little group, all naked, some of them with strips of white cloth tied around their black cocks.

Most us had never seen black people before, and particularly not naked black men, and certainly not naked black men with white streamers trailing from their cocks. Would some officer, we wondered, come along and tie white ribbons around our cocks?

We stared, mute and uneasy, as the black men shuffled around, silent, heads bowed mournfully, banded like birds, naked bodies as dark, shiny, and slick looking as molasses, glistening with the cold sweat of fear and humiliation.

Not sure of what kind of discipline we were now under, whether we could speak or even go to the toilet, but so puzzled at what we were seeing, we finally broke the silence, muttering and whispering among ourselves.

"What's the matter with them? Why have they got rags on their dicks?"

Some voice answered in a tense whisper: "They got the clap."

"Got what?"

"The clap. The clap. *Vee dee.*"

We stared at the black men with horror and distaste. They

were diseased, for Christ's sake. Good thing, we thought in our provincial way, we weren't going to be around them.

The African American man who came into Kirmser's, though, was nothing like those marked soldiers. Lucky said he was really bold to come into Kirmser's like he owned the place. There was something aloof, almost snotty, about him. He displayed a contempt for people, at least for us, a contempt that was evident in his most mundane gestures, like wiping his glasses. He kept a smirk on his face while doing this, flourishing his snow-white handkerchief, unfolding it, pursing his lips to blow a haughty bit of breath on each lens, like he was saying *Phew,* as if something stank, then wiping his glasses with slow, circular strokes before returning the handkerchief, folded again, to his breast pocket. Once the glasses were back on, he arched his neck, tilted his head back, and looked down his nose at the rest of us. It was the same look the Edstrom brothers used when they breezed in to look over the Saturday night crop.

The black man was always well dressed. Lulu Pulanski said he wore tailored clothes. The only time I saw him, he wore a pinstripe suit, vested, a shirt with French cuffs, gaudy, glittering cuff links and, strangest of all, black garters with snaps to hold up his socks. I could see those garters when he hitched up his pants to keep the crease from bagging at the knees while he sat at the bar. His hair was straight, pitch black, and shiny. He wore a large diamond ring on the little finger of his left hand, a watch with a gold metal band, and gold-rimmed glasses. When he lifted his upper lip to go *Phew,* I could see two big gold teeth.

We didn't like him, but we grudgingly credited him for his nerve in coming into Kirmser's, since during that era, African Americans ordinarily came downtown only to work, not to socialize. They shined shoes, carried luggage at the train station, cleaned the toilets, washed dishes, mopped floors, and if they were lucky, worked as waiters in a nice place like the dining room of the Ryan Hotel.

At first we thought he must have been a musician or entertainer of some kind, like Peg Leg Bates, to act so bold; he certainly was no boxer, no Brown Bomber like Joe Louis. We were disappointed, even a little irritated, to find out that he was a waiter on the Great Northern, working in the dining car on a run from Chicago to the West Coast.

His job didn't impress any of us, but the way he acted, it must have made him a man of some importance, perhaps in the black neighborhood up around Rondo Street. It was a steady job with the railroad, and the tips were said to be good.

He seemed unattractive to most of us, and only Betty Boop would have the nerve to suggest that maybe he had *hidden charms*. We didn't know much about black people, but we knew what Betty Boop meant—black men were said to be hung, with cocks as big as horses.

Pete refused to be impressed by big cocks in general, or horse cocks in particular. "What would you do with a cock that big?" he pooh-poohed. "Put it in a corner and throw kisses at it?"

We all agreed that we'd let Betty Boop find out. He was the size queen.

People who sat near the black gentleman at the bar sometimes spoke to him, but he never seemed interested in pursuing a conversation or making friends. He didn't seem to be cruising Kirmser's as much as to be shopping there, calmly making comparisons and searching for the right price.

As obnoxious as he was, he was the first black man to come into Kirmser's, and black or white, he belonged to the lodge. He was as queer as any of us; he was "one of the boys."

9

The Coney Island

ALL OF US who did not want to go home Saturday night after the bars closed came to the Coney Island, the "after hours" place on St. Peter Street in downtown St. Paul. The odor in the Coney Island was overwhelming, a mixture of cold grease, bitter coffee, sour beans, and raw onions, a stiffened, sudden assault on the nostrils, like smelling salts.

Featured on a big, blackened sheet grill that took up almost the whole greasy front window were rows of brown, sweaty, turd-shaped wieners that were cooked in close rank, in almost military precision, as if they were something glorious to behold.

As big as the Coney Island was, with its high old-fashioned pressed tin ceiling, its long low counter, its big booths, and its large seating area, and with all the customers passing through the front door, that thick, pungent odor always permeated the place, as if it had been mixed into the original plaster. Yet, the odor was not unpleasant, and was almost reassuring in its overwhelming familiarity.

All of the night owls, the lonesome soldiers between buses at the Greyhound bus depot, the old barflies, the drunks and the drifters, night workers getting off a late shift, people with time on their hands, queers on the prowl, easy women, the last bewildered celebrants of the city, all brought their particular hungers to the Coney Island. We were a mixed breed, and occasionally a straight man would make a play for one of the dykes. The woman, not about to enlighten him, would fend him off with as much tact and good nature as she could muster. For this reason, the dykes did not like to hang around the Coney Island. If they did come, even in pairs, they would sit with some of us so it looked like they were "with" somebody, because nice girls did not go unescorted into the Coney Island.

As rough and ready as the place was, as diverse as its customers were, I never saw a fight or heard a serious argument in the place, no matter how late the hour or how drunk the celebrants. The only unpleasantness I ever heard of was the night Ned got robbed in the toilet.

People were simply out for a good time, at worst for a thrill. For us, the Coney Island was the next-to-last opportunity to find a partner after Kirmser's closed. If nothing turned up at Kirmser's, and if the pickings were slim at the Coney Island, there was just one more place to go: Rice Park—The Last Chance.

Of course, for sheer escape, we always had the movies. They were the only drug we had. We didn't just go to the movies: we believed in them, abandoned ourselves to those enormous black and white gods who spoke, laughed, or sang on that large magic screen. They were glorious gods and goddesses: Cary Grant, Bette Davis, Mae West, Greta Garbo.

We sat, hushed, anxious to pick up every nuance, every gesture, every miracle that appeared on the screen. We were mesmerized, devout disciples, turning ourselves over body and soul to this magic. Held in the revolving jaws of the movie reel, we were pliable, easily manipulated, happily senseless. There in the dark, hunkered down in the safe, armed perimeters of our upholstered seats, part of the awesome, mindless anonymity of an audience, even a queer could imagine he was a part of that magic, no different than Tom Sawyer or Andy Hardy or the Katzenjammer Kids.

Movies gave us an enchanted, shared sensation, like sex without the body parts. It was something you could almost feel embrace you, a ghostly encounter, and we responded, tense, expectant, enthralled. We were manipulated toward the cinematic climax with emotions so strong, of such rarely touched depths, that we alternately laughed or cried until finally, at the end, an involuntary shudder and a profound relief spread through the audience like an immense ejaculation. It was escape. It made anything seem possible. It was a feeling so breathtaking we never wanted it to end.

The curtain closed and the house lights came on and we sat there momentarily stunned, let down, feeling as disappointed as Dorothy when she discovered the mechanical manipulations of the Wizard of Oz. We gathered up our gloves and scarves, looked about the bleak interior, shuffled into the aisles, a sullen, silent crowd jostling one another, coughing, blowing our noses, anxious to get outside and light up our cigarettes.

Movies were also the best escape from our parents, since most of us, after the war, had moved back home. Even Pete and Ned, as old as they were, with good jobs, and as independent as Pete was, still lived with Ned's parents. Living with our families necessitated some kind of strategy to keep them from finding out about the kind of lives we led.

A few of us even carried the subterfuge as far as gender switching when talking to friends in front of our parents. "He" became "she" and "him" became "her" and any particularly obnoxious guy became "that bitch." I hated the subterfuge. It was especially unsettling to hear Lucky, ordinarily the most guileless of men, slip into gender switching and do it so awkwardly, yet feel so clever about it.

"Everybody else does it," he'd protest when I complained. "It's kinda kicky."

He was right about that. Several of the guys at Kirmser's thought it was cute to refer to men as women, particularly people like Betty Boop and the Edstrom brothers. Ned had picked it up and did it perfectly, and even Pete did it once in a while, but only when he was cutting someone like Lulu Pulanski down to size.

Ned had an irritating habit when he would call from his parents' house, on nights when I was staying with Lucky, of first mentioning a man's name as he launched into a story, then switching gender as he got into the story.

"Remember Jim Anderson?" Ned would ask, then pause for a couple of seconds as if he were listening to the other party. "Oh, I was going to tell you about Jim, but since you mentioned *her* name, let me tell you what that bitch did the other night. She met this guy at the Coney Island. . . . "

Of course, he was still talking about Jim, but he had shifted gender. That kind of silliness set my teeth on edge. I had the uneasy feeling that there was a kind of self-deprecation in this charade, something degrading about our adopting the feminine position because we all knew that our culture believed that women were inferior to men. We all knew the standards. Men hunted. Men played baseball. They did not cry. Men were never friends with women. A real man would fuck a snake if someone held it still, but a real man would never let himself be fucked by anyone. Men worked and men went to war.

I remember an uncle of mine telling our family about his sixteen-year-old son, my cousin, who never told his family that he was having stomach cramps, but just went off to his room. When his mother finally found him, she called the doctor and they rushed him to the hospital for an emergency appendectomy.

"He never complained to anybody," my uncle boasted to all of us at Sunday dinner. He was clearly filled with enormous pride at his son's emerging manhood. "He just crawled off in a corner, like a dog."

Maybe we didn't meet these high standards, though we had standards of our own, but I didn't see any reason to make a joke of ourselves or of women by participating in this deceptive masquerade.

The gender-switching game seemed so obvious that I found it hard to believe Ned's parents were taken in by it, especially since Ned and Pete had lived with Ned's parents for fourteen years, all the while sleeping in the same double bed. Ned's father was retired and he drank too much. He had a bad back and a perfect memory, and he took these things into retirement with him. He was talkative, good natured, and kind, a steady beer drinker and a big sports fan who followed high school basketball in the winter and the St. Paul Saints baseball team in the summer. Neither Pete nor Ned gave a damn about baseball, but Pete kept up with the game and the standings just to be able to talk to the old man.

Although the family treated Ned and Pete's relationship as perfectly normal—Ned had even married once and Pete, of course, was fluent in baseball—Ned's father must have sensed something different about his son and his son's live-in buddy because the old man always referred to them as "the boys," though both Ned and Pete were in their early forties. It was as if the old man was granting them some kind of immunity by classifying them as "boys" rather than admitting to their manhood. There was never anything sly or sarcastic about the old man's references, nothing mean—he was never indirect and always obvious—but something desperately defensive. He was trying to make this marriage of two middle-aged men as innocent and unremarkable as two neighborhood boys playing marbles.

Underneath all his bluster and talk, the corny old jokes, the rambling discourses on baseball and all the baseball statistics he knew by heart, the problems with his back, his detailed recollections of the "good old days" when everyone "pulled together," behind all of his hearty references to "the boys," the old man sometimes seemed stunned, as if the breath had been knocked out of him. He seemed to sense some awful horror that he could neither identify nor dispel, something lurking about the house, something there in the dark that he dared not disturb.

If the relationship between Pete and Ned had puzzled and unnerved the father, Ned's mother thrived on it. She loved going places with them, being invited to the theater, the movies, out to dinner, for a Sunday ride. For Christmas and their birthdays she gave them leather gloves, monogrammed shirts, silk pajamas, Lena Horne and Glen Miller records, engraved cigarette lighters, cut glass decanters, and Russian Leather aftershave lotion.

They bought her expensive dresses, good jewelry, fine table linens, and the heaviest crystal. She ran their errands when they were at work. She cooked the dinners they liked. She ironed their shirts. She loved meeting their friends.

Whatever Pete and Ned's relationship had done to Ned's father, it made Ned's mother feel young again. She had entered the world of Peter Pan, where boys—good boys like her Ned and Pete—never grew up and never left home.

Once, when Ned was describing a dress that he and Pete had bought Ned's mother, Lulu let it be known that he had recently bought *his* mother a mink scarf.

"How grand," Pete later smirked, laughing at Pulanski's pretentions. "I suppose the old lady needs something warm while she's waiting in line in that drafty hall to go to the toilet."

I never heard Pete mention any of his family, except for a sister he seemed fond of and whom he still visited occasionally. She had instantly come to his defense the last time he'd visited her, when a couple of shirttail relatives asked Pete why he had never married. Before Pete could think of a snappy comeback, his sister asked, "Why the hell do you want to know that for?" She certainly sounded like Pete's sister, all right.

Pete and Ned had their bedroom and a little sitting room upstairs, and they had turned the basement into a recreation room, furnishing it comfortably with a built-in glass block bar, leather chairs, soft lights, knotty pine paneling, a new asphalt tile floor, and an old upright piano that they painted Chinese Red, a color that Ned said was "all the go." The old man was proud of what they had done. This was something boys were supposed to do. "We've got the finest rec room on Como Avenue," he boasted.

I always wondered how Pete and Ned got together in the first place, because they seemed so unalike. Pete was solid, substantial, sometimes pugnacious, blunt-faced and freckled. He just missed being homely. No one would ever guess that he was queer. Ned was what Lucky described as "flighty." He was small, cute, impulsive, and after a few drinks, kind of effeminate. Both pretended that they didn't give a damn what the other one did, and it was common gossip at Kirmser's that they stepped out on one another.

Lucky and I were at the Coney Island one night when we saw Ned sitting at the counter, talking to the guy next to him. Pete worked nights as a Linotype operator, so Ned had a lot of free evenings to himself. Ned saw us, but he didn't come over to our booth. He just winked at us and kept talking to the guy next to him. When the guy got up to go to the toilet, Ned followed him.

I wasn't surprised that Ned was cruising the Coney Island while Pete was at work. What surprised me was that he was cruising the Coney Island at all, after the trouble he had gotten into the previous year. A big, friendly drunk had winked at him in the toilet, and when Ned reached over to grope the guy's erection, the guy grabbed Ned by the wrist and threw him up against the wall.

"I oughta have ya arrested," the big guy growled, not sounding drunk at all, tightening his grip on Ned's wrist, releasing his hold only after Ned, with tears in his eyes, pleaded with him to let go. The man walked off with the cameo ring that Pete had given Ned, Ned's watch, and the six dollars in Ned's billfold.

Ned was still trying to figure out some way to keep all this from Pete—he'd already lied about losing the ring—when the guy called Ned's house early one morning a few days later, before Ned was even out of bed.

Pete heard Ned on the phone and wanted to know what was going on. Ned, in a panic because this guy had his phone number and might even know where he worked, confessed the whole thing to Pete: the guy winking, the threat, the money he'd lost, and the loss of the cameo ring that Pete had given him long ago, the first token of their partnership.

Pete was furious. "Why, that son of a bitch. What does he want now?"

"Twenty dollars," Ned gasped.

The guy had ordered Ned to meet him at the bar next door to the Coney Island. Ned agreed, but he didn't go alone. Pete and Lou went along. The plot was for Lou and Pete to pretend to be a couple of detectives that Ned had called. They wore their best Sunday suits. Lou, looking more like a gangster than a detective, entered the bar smoking one of his cheap cigars.

The big guy started to get up from the booth when he saw them come in, but Pete moved in quickly and pushed him back down, then slid in beside him, pinning him in the corner.

"He whined a little," Pete later told us, "and I don't know who was more scared, that fucking thief or us, pretending to be detectives."

The ring and the watch had been pawned and the pawn ticket thrown away, but Lou had been smart enough, as soon as they sat down, to demand to see the guy's identification so they could track him down if they had to.

"Beat it before we run you in," Pete ordered, imitating a tough guy in a James Cagney movie.

Ned hadn't been bothered since. Now here he was, cruising the Coney Island as if nothing had ever happened, that telltale pink flush on his face, a sure sign that he was drunk and horny.

That particular incident didn't seem to damage their relationship. They had been together fourteen years, outlasting and sometimes outmaneuvering the competition. They were proud of their record.

Pete hated to sound sentimental, but he finally told me how

he and Ned had met. It was on the Como-Harriet streetcar line one summer. This was the line that ran along Como Avenue in St. Paul over to Lake Harriet in Minneapolis, and it was the line that was known for years to queers in both cities as the "Homo Chariot."

It was not only an easy play on words, but "Homo Chariot" also was an appropriate designator because the notorious old Edstrom brothers lived along the line. One Halloween, the brothers, dressed in drag and with two other old aunties, boarded the Como-Harriet, heading for a big drag party in Minneapolis. Dressed in elaborate antebellum costumes like something out of *Gone with the Wind,* their hoopskirts were too big for them all to fit into their car, so they were forced to take the trolley.

Halloween was the night to howl. Like Winter Carnival, much mischief was forgiven or overlooked. Men dressing as women would ordinarily be arrested, but not on Halloween.

They got on the streetcar, wobbling along on high heels, big picture hats askew on their heads, holding their great hoopskirts aloft. They brandished their parasols, screeching in mock terror as they minced their way down the aisle as the trolley jerked along.

Pete was taking this same Como-Harriet car home on the night he met Ned. He had caught the one o'clock lineup and he was sitting there, waiting for the trolley to take off, feeling sorry for himself because he was so damn lonely in the city. Kirmser's wasn't in existence then, at least not as a queer bar, and Pete had spent a lousy night popping in and out of bars, talking baseball with regular guys and feeling terrible. He knew what he was looking for, but he had no idea where to find it.

Just as the streetcar jerked into action, rumbling along its tracks, Pete slumped down in his seat, staring out the window, watching some silly bastard run frantically as he tried to catch the streetcar. It was some young blond guy, apparently drunk, bounding along, laughing and hollering for the conductor to wait for him.

The kid finally caught up with the trolley, jumped up on the back platform, and lurched into the enclosed car. He flung himself down into the first empty space. It was the seat next to Pete.

"Boy, I thought I'd missed it," he laughed, his face flushed.

"When he smiled at me," Pete told me, "and looked at me with those big, blue eyes, I was hooked." Then, as if embarrassed at such a sentimental story, Pete laughed and added, "and I've been with that dizzy blond ever since."

That was fourteen years ago and they were still together. Despite the odds against them, in spite of the church, the laws, the customs, the neighbors, Pete's family, despite all the pressures and all the temptations, their particular alliance had survived. And, even if it was no longer a romance, it had remained a miracle.

Pete had invited a minister from Red Wing, a man who showed up in Kirmser's whenever he could find an excuse to travel alone to the city, to one of their parties. The minister was a balding, portly old rascal, with plum-colored lips, sly, hooded eyes, and a face full of varicose veins. He looked like a character right out of Charles Dickens.

On his little excursions into Kirmser's, he'd take off his black clerical garb and change into what he called his "lounging clothes": slacks, sport coat, and sport shirt. Most of us in Kirmser's were shocked when we first learned that he was a minister, and Red Larson was dumbfounded at the revelation that the minister was a Lutheran, like Red.

Pete, however, had taken a shine to the old boy, perhaps out of some mischievous interest, and he treated him like a celebrity, buying him drinks, always inquiring kindly about his health, his trip, his family.

The minister had come to the party at Pete's insistence. All of us were gathered in the basement recreation room, with Ned playing the piano and his mother running in and out with bottles of beer, bowls of popcorn, and peanuts. The minister started to leave early, making excuses about a busy schedule, a slight cold, a long trip, obviously anxious to get back to Kirmser's before the bar closed and he missed his last chance to pick up a trick. It was foolish of him to lie about it. We all knew by the next night that he had gone back to Kirmser's.

Pete kept a straight face through all these protests. He helped the old goat into his overcoat, handed him his hat, and cordially offered to walk him upstairs and out to his car. As the minister turned to wish us all goodnight, Pete placed one arm around the minister's shoulders, gave him a conspiratorial hug, grinned, and petitioned loud enough for the whole crowd to hear.

"Pray for us, Revie, pray for us and get all of us bitches into heaven."

The old hypocrite blushed at this cavalier treatment, turning more purple than usual. His dimples disappeared dourly into his jowls, but he recovered from his brief dismay, laughed, and blandly replied, "My goodness . . . Yes, of course."

We were glad he was gone. We sat down to eat and afterward, our bellies full and our spirits high, we gathered around the old piano to salute an absentee brother, one who had never been invited in the first place: the piss-elegant Lulu Pulanski. We went through several loud, rousing choruses of

> You can bring Pearl
> She's a darn nice girl
> But don't bring Lulu . . .
> You can bring Rose
> With the turned-up nose
> But don't bring Lulu . . .

Ned's mother came in to clear away the dirty dishes as we were singing, and we coaxed her to join us in a couple of choruses, though she pretended dismay at such shabby treatment of Lulu, whoever the poor girl was.

10

Flaming Youth

*F*LAMING YOUTH HAD A SECRET LIFE. It wasn't his homosexual activity, nothing as obvious as that. The man we all knew as the biggest whore in town, an icon of homosexuality in St. Paul, the man who traveled through the toilets of the city like the convict Jean Valjean traveled through the sewers of Paris, this man was a gentleman. It was true. The biggest whore in town was a gentleman. Joe was that rare human being, no man's toad and no one's master. He had hidden charms. The body had a soul.

I learned this when I got to know him better, running into him around town and having coffee with him, after the attack in Kirmser's. He wasn't the one-dimensional character we had all assumed when we passed our superficial judgment on him, when we dubbed him Flaming Youth, our folk hero, the king of the cruisers.

I used to watch him as he sat in Kirmser's at the bar, usually by himself. He had a shiny bald head and a thick, gray moustache, and black hair bristled in his ears. Sitting there in his familiar winter costume—navy peacoat, black turtleneck sweater, brown corduroy pants, boots, navy blue wool watch cap—he appeared rough looking, common and confident like a capable old sailor.

Everyone knew Joe. He was friendly with all of us. We spoke to him and he smiled and nodded. He was pointed out to people new to Kirmser's. "That's Flaming Youth," we'd proudly announce, pointing to our landmark. Joe always smiled back. Forty years old and still called "Flaming Youth." Joe accepted the title. That's the way it was.

Flaming Youth had one natural enemy: Betty Boop.

"He's all over, like horseshit," Betty Boop would complain whenever he and Joe would cross tracks in the same toilet.

Betty Boop really had no reason to complain. Even he admitted that whenever they found themselves on the same hunting grounds, Joe graciously disappeared, leaving the field to Betty Boop or any other queer who came by. When Betty Boop came swishing into the Montgomery Ward's Midway toilet or the Golden Rule basement rest room to find Joe already there, nonchalantly smoking a cigarette, waiting for the kill, even if he already had his man marked, Joe invariably acknowledged the competition with a discreet, good-natured nod. Then he would bow out, and resume his hunt in less productive but unoccupied territory like the bus depot, the basement toilet in the public library, or the second-floor washroom in the Bremer Arcade.

On the other hand, Betty Boop, as we well knew, would take over a toilet, practically hissing at the competition if there was any. Then he'd stand there forever, combing and recombing his hair, patting the curls into place, chain-smoking cigarettes, peering into the mirror to monitor the action and check the baskets of any men behind him.

I'd always thought that the only guys from Kirmser's who cruised tea rooms were Flaming Youth, Betty Boop, and maybe the Edstrom brothers. I learned that others occasionally checked out these places, although they were reluctant to admit it. If any were caught by Betty Boop, hovering near a notorious tea room, they made elaborate excuses for being there.

Competition apparently was fierce in the toilets, often from people who would never dare come into Kirmser's or who had never even heard of the place. One of them, an old-timer whom

Joe once pointed out to me, was a decrepit, dirty old man who always carried a shopping bag full of his shoes when he cruised the Golden Rule basement men's room. He stayed there for hours, enthroned in a booth with a lemon-sized hole cut out of the wall between his wooden stall and the next, waiting patiently waiting for someone to shove his stiff staff of life through the glory hole. To avoid suspicion by anyone who might be checking the time each occupant spent in a stall, the old man would slip off one pair of shoes and put on a different pair about every half an hour. He had a pair of brown shoes, a pair of black shoes, and a pair of grubby boots.

Joe had spent one morning browsing around the bargain basement in the Golden Rule, keeping watch on the men's room after he'd seen the old man with the shopping bag go inside. He timed the old guy at an hour and a half and the man was still in there when Joe left, probably starting a new round of shoe exchanges. Joe was highly amused at the old man's ingenuity.

The competition did get checked out at times. Betty Boop once took the license number of a Lincoln Zephyr that he'd seen parked alongside Rice Park a couple of nights one summer. The driver was cruising strangers who walked past, and he finally picked up a kid who was leaning against the iron railing rubbing his crotch. Betty Boop called the license bureau to get the name and address of the car's owner, then checked the city directory and discovered that the owner was a big shot at the *Pioneer Press.* None of us, except Red and Chester, who worked there and were shocked at the news, had ever heard of him, but he had an important title.

I no longer worked there, but I walked by the *Pioneer Press* building once after that incident just to look up at it and marvel at the secret inside. A big shot like that. Just like us. I wondered what he looked like.

As I got to know Flaming Youth better, I began to look forward to seeing him around town on Saturday afternoons after I got off work. I realized that he didn't mix very much with any of the other guys in Kirmser's, although he was friendly with all of us. The Edstrom brothers knew him from way back, in the Roaring Twenties, when Joe first came out. They had given him his nickname, but he never went to their drag parties. He always talked to them, even camped it up with them a little, but he never ran around with them. He was about the same age as Pete and Ned—and one of the few people Pete treated as an equal—but he was never at their parties. He didn't pal around with Lucky or Dale, he had little to say to Lulu Pulanski, and he kept his distance from Mick Flaherty, as we all did. He sometimes sparred good-naturedly with Betty Boop and some of the girls.

If he had a real friend, a confidante, at Kirmser's, it was Lou. The two of them sometimes talked quietly up at Joe's end of the bar, shaking their heads and laughing at the peculiarities of life. They would sit there, balanced comfortably on their bar stools, as Lou, in his shiny old blue serge, blew great, gray clouds of foul-smelling cigar smoke, and Joe, in his navy blue peacoat, smoked his Camels. The two of them were like an old vaudeville team, the Blue Brothers, troupers in a hazy blue spotlight, who had traveled everywhere, seen everything, and were surprised at nothing.

Both were realists, but while Lou's outlook was rather cold or at best ironic, Joe tended to view life with an amused tolerance, as if it were just a Laurel and Hardy comedy. I often thought of his wry, accurate description of us as "tainted meat," the one phrase that summed up the way society saw us better than anything I'd ever heard.

In all the time I knew him, all the nights in Kirmser's, all of our Saturday afternoons together, all of our talks about books, movies, and music, I never knew where Joe lived, never knew what company he worked for, never knew if he had a family or where he was born. All I knew was that he lived in a basement apartment and had no phone. I never even knew that he had a partner until I accidentally met both of them one day in Walgreen's. The only relative he had ever mentioned was a sister in Wisconsin whom he sometimes visited, a sister he seemed as fond of as Pete was of his sister. Sisters, I was beginning to realize, were among the best of women.

We talked about movies and our favorite stars, like Bette Davis, Myrna Loy, Mae West, W. C. Fields, Judy Garland, James Cagney, and Laurel and Hardy. We always alerted one another to movies where our favorite wisecracking comediennes had small roles, the lesser-known favorites like Zazu Pitts, Patsy Kelly, Eve Arden, Joan Davis, and that wonderful old dragon, Dame Edna Mae Oliver.

Joe sometimes tried to talk to me about music, but I was hopeless. I had little coordination, no rhythm, and I was no musician. I had a tin ear and two lead feet, and music had never been part of our lives at home. We had an old phonograph, but nobody collected records. Once in a while my dad would get a little sentimental and play the "Marine Corps Hymn" or "Home on the Range," two of the few records we did have. We never ventured much beyond that.

Joe and I discovered, however, that we liked the same writers: John Steinbeck, Sherwood Anderson, Mark Twain, and Sinclair Lewis, writers Joe described as "the salt of the earth," American writers who wrote honestly and with great passion about America.

We'd stop for coffee at the Golden Rule basement lunch counter, at Mickey's Diner, and sometimes we'd walk up to the YMCA and take over a couple of stools at the tiny corner lunch counter outside the cafeteria.

"Nothing doing here," Joe said once when he saw me looking over a couple of fellows in the cafeteria line. "This place is as dull as a nunnery."

That's the reputation it had. Lulu Pulanski had stayed there after getting out of the army, renting one of the sleeping rooms upstairs, a nicer place than his old tenement, but he still had to go down the hall to the toilet, just like home. Nobody cruised the St. Paul YMCA, not like the Lawson YMCA in Chicago, where Lulu had stayed overnight coming home on furlough.

Lulu said, "People roamed the halls all night at the Lawson Y. Room doors were left ajar, sometimes with a naked occupant stretched out on the bed. Showers ran constantly in the big shower room. One guy took so many showers he looked waterlogged."

Nothing like that happened at the St. Paul YMCA. It was typical of St. Paul, where things were the way they should be, that there was no hanky-panky in the YMCA. That suited Joe and me fine. It was a pleasant, out-of-the-way retreat in the middle of the day.

I usually suggested the coffee. Joe would go for the coffee when it was suggested, but I soon realized that he viewed my attempts to add doughnuts to our coffee stop as a trifle extravagant.

One Saturday afternoon when we hiked over to the YMCA and settled in at the cozy lunch counter for coffee, Joe asked if I'd ever read anything by Willa Cather. I'd never heard of her, but Joe was sure I'd like her.

"She writes as well as any man and much better than Hemingway, although she's not as popular now as she once was."

Hemingway was the only respected author I had ever heard Joe criticize.

"Something doesn't ring true about him," Joe said. "Some kind of pose, some affectation that gums up his stories. Hemingway is just a debutante at the dance. Cather, Steinbeck, and Mark Twain make the music."

I looked at Joe. I'd never heard him talk that way at Kirmser's. I read *My Antonia,* went back for *O Pioneers!* and then checked out *One of Ours.* Joe was right. I'd never read anything so good in my life. I couldn't analyze my reaction to Cather's work. It was a wonderful feeling, something as thrilling as my first taste of Coca-Cola.

One summer day when I was a child, I went into the St. Croix drugstore after swimming in the river. I was standing barefoot and small by the magazine rack, afraid to touch anything, but drinking in all the beautiful sights: *Liberty Magazine, Colliers, The Saturday Evening Post, Esquire.* Jake Wilfahrt came in and slouched over at the marble soda fountain.

"Gimme a Coke and some Planter's Peanuts," he ordered.

I stood transfixed, still and silent, a witness to this flagrant outrage: ugly, big-assed Jake Wilfahrt devouring tiny, crisp little peanuts and washing them down with Coca-Cola. The words were magic and music. They promised *The Pause That Refreshes.* Pretty girls with apple-red cheeks advertised its presence everywhere.

Not until a year later, when I got my paper route, did I finally taste the glories of Coca-Cola. It was the stuff I'd dreamed of.

Yes, that was it. Willa Cather was the Coca-Cola of writers, an American original, keeping the promise, bringing the nectar and the wisdom of the gods to even the smallest and the meekest among us. To Joe, she was music. To me, she was Coca-Cola.

Joe also mentioned a book about "people like us" called *The Scarlet Pansy.* It was a book about queer men, not like *The Well of Loneliness,* which was a book about lesbians, a book I had tried to read but found too dull to finish. It was about rich, unhappy English lesbians, nothing like the cheerful girls I knew at Kirmser's. *The Scarlet Pansy,* while it was about rich, unhappy English queers, was not quite so dull, because it had the added attraction of being filled with scenes of sometimes covert, yet sometimes hot, man-to-man sex.

There was a drollness about Joe that was surprising in its insight. We were in Kirmser's one night when John Clark, a kid who worked as a short-order cook, came in, bubbling with excitement. He'd met this "really good-looking guy" on the bus coming back from a visit to Rochester. The guy was coming to

St. Paul to look for work, and John let him move in rent-free with him "just until he gets a job."

Joe cocked an eyebrow.

"That long?" he asked sympathetically, and we all laughed.

It had never occurred to me that anyone whose life seemed so public would have a private life. Joe did. He had a partner of several years, and his partner was not some rough trade or some dumb, husky kid. Joe's partner was a gentle, bright, and very funny guy who made a precarious living designing stained glass windows for churches. Joe looked after him with great consideration, cheerful affection, and pride in his talent. He even shared with his partner some of the tricks that he picked up.

Joe's partner never came into Kirmser's. Joe's partner was leery that some "ecclesiastic," as he lightly referred to them, might spot him going into a queer bar and cancel an order. When I saw Joe with a stranger in Walgreen's one afternoon, I was hesitant to speak to him, but Joe spotted me and he and the stranger came over.

"This is my partner," he said without mentioning a name, and then added, after an awkward pause, "This is Rick, my sidekick."

Joe and Rick were both music lovers, classical music, and they spent many evenings at concerts, recitals, and, whenever possible, the opera. Joe even had a special wardrobe for concert going, a black Chesterfield coat that he'd found at the Salvation Army, a white silk scarf, and a gray felt hat, a fairly good fit. The hat had been left behind in Joe's apartment by a married trick who had beaten a hasty retreat one afternoon when Joe's partner unexpectedly showed up.

Joe's notoriety for cruising toilets didn't bother me too much. After all, I'd met a man in a washroom once. I'd picked up an ensign in the bright, spacious men's room in the lower level of the Palmer House in Chicago. I was in yeoman school at the time, on weekend liberty, and the ensign and I found ourselves with side-by-side hard-ons at the polished white urinals.

He was an officer and I was just an enlisted man, so he made the first move, winking a big slaphappy wink. When I smiled back, he led me jubilantly off in search of a nice, quiet hotel room. He was drunk, gloriously drunk, with the blind, magnificent confidence that only a drunk or a prince can have.

"We're going to have the time of our lives tonight," he promised as we lurched joyously along the street, in high good humor, clutching one another around the waists for support.

I'd had a few drinks but I wasn't drunk, and his good-natured exuberance alarmed me. "What about the Shore Patrol?" I asked.

He took the question in stride, considered it a minute as something foreign and completely inappropriate, and then, unshaken in his assurance and magnanimous in his anticipated pleasure, he took the whole Shore Patrol into our confidence. "The Shore Patrol? Well, okay, let's hear it for the Shore Patrol! Three cheers for the Shore Patrol! Hip, hip, hooray for the Shore Patrol!"

We were only a block from the Palmer House, arms encircling one another's waists, beaming with pleasure at our newfound alliance, a little unsteady on our feet but determined to find that quiet, little hotel. When two dignified matrons in heavy fur coats approached us, seeing this joyful comradeship between two young men in uniform, they smiled benignly just as the ensign reached across my waist with his free left hand and playfully squeezed my cock. Their smiles vanished and their look of shock and horror danced grotesquely before my eyes as we staggered onward toward our night of carnal joy.

I thought often about that night, the way it began, when I heard people at Kirmser's talking about Joe. The fact was, most of us had done at least once or twice what Joe did on a regular basis—picked up men in toilets—and the only difference between those who disapproved of Joe's flagrant behavior and Joe himself was the openness with which Joe lived that part of his life. He wasn't ashamed of his behavior. It was a part of who he was, and he accepted it. That's what I admired about Joe, the way he lived his life not in defiance or in spite of anyone else, but only in the fulfillment of his own desires, his own dreams.

11

Winter Carnival

WINTER CARNIVAL BROUGHT PEOPLE, money, and excitement into the city. A few out-of-town queers even managed to slip into Kirmser's, eagerly crossing into our forbidden world, bold and almost reckless away from their small-town prisons. There were usually a few school teachers, students, white-collar workers, and even an occasional minister or rancher. They filtered into Kirmser's, bundled up in overcoats, galoshes, earmuffs, and hats. Their eyes were bright, their cheeks flushed, and they were agog with anticipation, anxious to sample for a night the forbidden pleasures that they dared not even hint of knowing about in their offices, classrooms, lodges, and granges back home.

Winter Carnival brought good business into Kirmser's, but Mr. and Mrs. Kirmser never hired extra help. They were too frugal to pay someone else or too reluctant to let any outsider discover the kind of crowd they harbored. The two of them just worked harder. Mrs. Kirmser seemed to thrive on the activity. She busied herself from table to bar to booth, calling out orders to Mr. Kirmser, who stoically endured all the commotion from his long, narrow sanctuary behind the bar. Mrs. Kirmser still exchanged brief but pleasant greetings with her regular customers, but there was no time for chitchat during carnival. She was too busy taking orders, serving drinks, cleaning up, making change, and checking ID's to make sure the strangers were old enough to drink. She ran the place with precision.

It was not like the Ryan Hotel bar, where the Winter Carnival crowd was so thick that when I once stopped by with Meg and her boyfriend, it was impossible to get near the bar. You could stand in that crowd in the Ryan Hotel bar all night and not get a drink. The Ryan Hotel was a madhouse during Winter Carnival. The old hotel, a dirty, red brick Victorian Gothic, had once been grand, but now it was down at the heels, its marble steps worn and its carpets faded. It no longer commanded respect or even courtesy, so it was an easy mark for the noisy, boisterous carnival crowd, who spilled beer in the lobby, ground out their cigarettes on the carpets, romped through the wide halls, and dropped water balloons from upper-floor windows.

In Kirmser's, no matter how busy it was, Mrs. Kirmser never relaxed her vigilance. She could always spot an empty glass or an empty hand and she promptly zeroed in on the freeloaders. "Vot you vant to drink?" she would ask the culprit. There were no free rides, no window shopping in Kirmser's.

We clustered cozily together during carnival. The place was steamy with excitement, and we savored the body heat and the "accidental" groping: a hand brushed against your crotch or glided along your butt. We drank in the scent of wet wool, beer, whisky, Old Spice, Seaforth, the keen bitter tang of cigarette smoke, and the clammy stench of cold feet. Each time the front door opened, letting in a blast of ice cold air, eyes turned, heads swiveled, backs arched for a better view. Conversations faltered as each newcomer was appraised, categorized, and then either dismissed as uninteresting, unattainable, or suspicious, or noted as a possible prospect.

Saturday night during the 1946 Winter Carnival was the biggest night of the whole festival. Nobody worked on Sunday and the weekenders from out of town began showing up. Most of us regulars were already there. The Three Kind Mice had come early to get a good booth; Louie had brought a friend along from the university—an eager little redhead—and the minister from Red Wing, the old hypocrite, was buying them drinks. Flo and Miriam ducked in and out, carrying their ice skates, and Chester was in and out a couple of times looking for Red Larson. Dale was talking to his school teacher friend from Wisconsin, and two hairdressers arrived from Minneapolis, their hair plastered rigidly into neat little waves, as yellow as lemon pie. Flaming Youth had stopped in for a drink before going back out to check his "trap line," as he called it; Pete and Ned were talking to a small band of celebrants from Duluth, and Lulu and his partner stopped in after a dinner party. Lou was talking to a trucker from Fargo, while Betty Boop positioned himself near the toilet to check out the statistics on any interesting newcomers. I was delighted to see, amid all the hubbub, the Guy with Crabs, the bar's outcast, now radiant with joy as he escaped out the front door, tugging a husky young farmer by the arm. Lucky and I were talking to Tony at the bar. Even Wayne had allowed Bart to bring him along for the occasion, and Mother Jerusalem managed to make it, half an hour before midnight, arriving breathless and anxious after taking his fiancé home and then coming all the way back downtown by streetcar.

The 1946 carnival was more exciting than usual. It was a double celebration. We had won the war and the carnival was back. The city even renamed that year's revived event the Victory Carnival. We toasted Harry Truman, a "regular guy," as president. "He never even went to college," we solemnly reminded one another.

While admiring Truman as the Common Man, we perversely looked forward to all the royal pomp and pageantry of carnival: the Queen of the Snows, King Boreas, the parades, the platoons of princesses from every small town in the state, and the Vulcans.

The Vulcans were the "fire gods" who dethroned the winter royalty at the end of carnival, signifying the end of winter. They were masked young men, outfitted in crimson capes and black masks—all of them honored war veterans this year—who leaped on and off their fire truck as they chased women and girls through the streets. They rode imperiously around town on their bright red fire engine, clanging the bell, leaping on and off the running boards to dart into vestibules, stores, lobbies, even elevators, grabbing women, kissing them, then smearing their foreheads with grease paint, signifying the mark of the Vulcan. Being singled out for a Vulcan kiss, as messy and as crude as it was, was considered an honor for any woman.

Aunt Mary, who had always worked downtown, recalled with mock indignation and real pride the two times, sixteen years apart, that she had been caught, kissed, and branded by the Vulcans. It was great sport to watch the Vulcans run down their quarry, chasing, cornering, hugging, kissing, and branding them amid the hollering, the laughter, the squeals, and the screams of bystanders and the victims.

These ribald scenes set the tone for Winter Carnival, a time for grab-ass and make-out, for drunken parties, for snake dancing through the stores and streets, for fireworks, for pissing in the snow. It was the approved method for citizens to let off steam after a long winter, before they settled in for the somber days of Lent. Winter Carnival came at a time, early in the new year, when business was slow, after the Christmas buying spree and before the spring season. The carnival was good for business. It goosed up the city.

The gang at Kirmser's loved it. We were warmed by the crowds, the intimacy, the comradeship of carnival. We wanted, like everyone else, to have fun. We became careless, sometimes even rash, in our approaches and our confidences. Some of us even gave our full names when we met the out-of-town visitors, and if the visitors were desperate or smitten enough, they sometimes disclosed their real addresses or phone numbers.

We all prepared for carnival in our individual way. Flaming Youth took part of his vacation then because cruising was at its peak; Pulanski bought a baby blue cashmere sweater, a much-talked-about extravagance, typical for the piss-elegant Lulu; the old Edstrom brothers had invited out-of-town guests; Dale chipped in with Lucky and me to rent a room for an after-hours party at the Ryan Hotel; and Dickie Grant showed up in Kirmser's wearing a big, red, wool sweater with a reindeer pattern, with red rouged cheeks to match.

Lucky scolded him for the rouge and made him go into the toilet and wash it off. Dickie reluctantly obeyed. He hated to use the toilet and only went when he could no longer avoid the trip. He was too embarrassed to share the trough urinal with anyone. He always huddled in the corner over that one open stool to take his pee. It was a big joke with the rest of us who had been in the service and so were used to the lack of privacy in toilets and the showers. When Dickie came out, pale and abashed, he confessed that he had just wanted to look healthy and rosy cheeked, "like a skier," he said.

Even during Winter Carnival, we observed the rules. There were never any overt signs of affection between men in Kirmser's, although a good-natured bear hug was acceptable, as it would be anywhere else. But a kiss between men, or an embrace, even in Kirmser's, was unthinkable, a deadly, ancient taboo. We all knew what the taboos were, from generation to generation, as well as the penalties for straying: banishment, disgrace, unemployment, ridicule, beatings, prison. Men simply did not show affection for one another, not even homosexuals. Not even in Kirmser's. Not even during Winter Carnival.

We got by with furtive but revealing glances, a sly wink, with arms around one another's shoulders, nothing frontal but side by side, a "buddy" hug. We got by with an exchange of smiles and, once in a great while, we might risk a surreptitious pinch on the ass.

In the hubbub of Winter Carnival, there was occasional goosing as well as ass pinching. The goosing, the pinch on the ass, even a quick squeeze of someone's balls, was acceptable. It could be passed off as crude male roughhousing, locker-room fun, but there was no way to exonerate such a damning action as a genuine caress, any real affection between men. Such an action took you across a barrier that forever stripped you of your manhood.

Codes may have been relaxed during Winter Carnival, and some of the rules overlooked, but the only time I ever saw a customer get out of line in Kirmser's, other than the night the straight thugs beat up Flaming Youth, was that gloriously busy Saturday night during the 1946 carnival.

The Edstrom brothers had come in with two other old aunties shortly before closing time, and they positioned themselves in the rear of the place, by the jukebox, to look over the prospects. They were dressed in their usual Saturday night finery, and they were a little giddy with the carnival spirit. Picking the perfect moment when the jukebox was changing records after a rousing "Beer Barrel Polka" by the Andrews Sisters, when there was a lull in the music and the conversation was low, Laverne Edstrom suddenly screeched out his challenge: "I'll suck any cock in the house!"

There he stood, a bony old fart, his cheeks flushed or rouged, that sharp little face as predatory as an eagle's, eyes glittering behind his gold-rimmed glasses, a triumphant smirk on his face. The raucous bar crowd was stunned into silence. We were frozen, waiting for the thunderbolt. For, shocked as we were at Laverne's outburst, we were mesmerized at the thought of what Mrs. Kirmser would do.

We watched, breathless, as Mrs. Kirmser, her back arched and her shoulders thrown back, in her usual nunlike black, waddled grimly through the crowd to confront the culprit. She stood there, just inches away from Laverne, one arm on her ample hip, and she raised her other arm right up under Edstrom's nose to shake a thick forefinger at him. "Tch! Tch!" she scolded. "Sich langwidge." Then, to our astonishment, she went back about her business, simply walked away and started picking up empty beer bottles from nearby tables.

The Edstroms and their guests chose this time to make their exits; to stick around now would be anticlimactic. As they made their way through the crowd, still smirking, triumphant and gleeful at the sensation they had caused, people fell back, silently making room, avoiding any contact, any brush at all with the offenders.

That same Saturday night, at the height of the festivities, Red Larson was caught cornholing a guy in the back seat of his dad's car. Red's brief story in the paper referred to the arrest of the two men for indecent conduct, a term that could cover anything from swearing in public to pissing in the snow. Red spent a couple of months in the workhouse and he lost his job. After the workhouse, he was put on probation, and he never came into Kirmser's again.

Chester talked to him on the phone a couple of times, once suggesting they meet in Kirmser's some night.

Red was flustered. "I can't go," he insisted.

Assuming Red was too embarrassed to come back into Kirmser's, Chester suggested they meet instead at Matt Weber's. But Red couldn't go there, either, at least not with Chester, who was horrified when Red finally blurted out that he was forbidden to associate with "known perverts" like Chester and anyone else who frequented Kirmser's.

Shortly after Chester told me this, I saw Red in Walgreen's one afternoon. He'd always been so buoyant before, so eager to please, a beefy, good-natured guy, a little goofy sometimes, one of those sexless, decent sort of men often described as "good eggs."

I had expected him to be more serious, bitter even, but I wasn't prepared for the transformation he had obviously gone through in the intervening months. He couldn't look at me when I spoke to him, and though he talked at me, his gaze kept sliding away from my nose to my jacket to my shoes. Anxiously, he kept looking out of the corners of his eyes, as if he was afraid someone was watching us.

I'd always thought of him as two-dimensional before, a man with two red masks: the jolly mask, and the deeper red mask he wore when he was embarrassed. Now, he had a new look, and it wasn't a mask; this was the real Red Larson, unmasked, his pudgy, colorless face a dead man's face, embalmed, expressionless, frozen in the past.

Shocked at what I saw, I called him by name to get his attention, hoping to say something encouraging to him. When he heard his name, he obediently jerked his head up and I looked into his eyes and then quickly glanced away, looking down at my shoes and fervently wishing that I hadn't seen what I saw. Someone should have had the decency to close this dead man's eyes.

I prayed; I prayed in earnest, not for Red Larson, exactly, but for myself. I thanked God that I hadn't been caught and publicly exposed as a queer, that my name had never gotten into the papers, that I had never been imprisoned, a queer penned up among an army of restless, ruthless heterosexuals. I thanked God that my undesirable discharge had never made the news.

Red had been to Lucky's house and to parties at Pete and Ned's, but neither Lucky's mother nor Ned's parents seemed aware of Red's arrest. It was unlikely that, even if they had read the brief story or understood what it meant, they would have connected that monster Harold E. Larson—arrested for indecent conduct—with that cheeky, homely Red Larson, who had been such a welcome guest in their homes.

Red's parents reacted strangely to his arrest, unlike anything we would have expected. They didn't throw Red out, as we all thought they would. Instead, his mother drove Red downtown each week to see his probation officer, because she wasn't about to let Red use the family car again. And, Chester told us, Red's father angrily blamed the whole horrible affair on the army, on the war. Wars did strange things to men, segregated by themselves, facing death, cut off from their families, without women.

That's how Red's father saw it. "The war did this to Red," he insisted.

We were surprised, even a little uneasy, at this odd turn of events. It wasn't what we had expected at all. The fear of rejection by our parents if they ever found out about us had haunted our minds so long that we had turned it into gospel. When it never happened to Red, we almost felt cheated. Wasn't it what we deserved? Right or wrong, wasn't that the way things went? Our assumptions about our world were turned upside down, and we didn't know how to react.

Red's partner that night, the drunk he was caught fucking, turned out to be a married man with four kids. He was one of those poor, anonymous men who haunted Rice Park—where Red had picked him up—only in the dead of night, even in the chill of winter, and only when they were drunk enough to later claim that they didn't know what was happening. The married man escaped with a fine. The law had decided that he was the victim.

This astonished me. I couldn't figure it out. The married man had been the passive partner. Red had been the active one. Didn't society always have more contempt for a passive man, one who would allow himself to be fucked? Was being drunk, as long as you were ostensibly straight, an excuse for any trouble you got into? Was being married the best defense?

I talked to Flaming Youth about it at Kirmser's one night, figuring that Joe's experience with all kinds of trade might provide some insight into the situation. He grinned when I asked him.

"Being straight, saying you're straight, doesn't mean a thing," he said. "Some of the toughest guys I've picked up beat me to the floor when I got them home."

"Beat you to the floor?" I repeated, not quite sure what he meant.

"Yeah. One of them even came already greased up, ready for action, with Vaseline in his ass."

12

The Picture in the Window

WHEN THE WEATHER WARMED UP in the spring, Lucky invited Pete, Ned, and me on a Sunday trip to Red Wing. We planned an all-day affair, leaving right after Lucky brought his mother home from church, and returning early Sunday evening. It was a pleasant day for an outing: clear, sunny, fresh, and full of promise as the drab country turned green again with that earthen, urgent recklessness of spring. The most important thing we had to think about was where we would eat lunch. We agreed that if we saw any roadhouse that looked "kicky," we would stop for a beer and look over the "local talent," as Pete called them.

In Red Wing, Lucky parked the car down by the river and we walked around town, our jackets open, feeling the warmth of the sun on our backs. As we looked into store windows, we stopped to make fun of the portraits in a photographer's window: garishly colored graduation pictures; the well-fed look of a local bride; an old farm couple celebrating an anniversary, looking appropriately grim at the prospect. As I looked among the wedding pictures, the stiff graduation poses, the glazed expressions of the brides and grooms, I saw a picture of "Friend," Friend from the navy, smiling out at the world with his bride.

Surprised and pleased at this discovery, I almost blurted out, "Hey, I know this guy," but I didn't speak. Caution warned me to be silent. "Friend" (the only name I ever had for him) was part of my navy experience, the ugly part, when we were briefly bunkmates in the isolation barracks, waiting to be drummed out of the navy.

There he was, Friend, my fellow inmate, now looking so forthright, so proud and respectable, a young farmer in a rented tux, his blond hair parted meticulously on one side, clear eyed, clean shaven, a model of respectability. His bride was pretty enough, except for a kind of stubborn set to her jaw. They were the handsomest couple in the window. Off to a beautiful new life. I wondered if he had pissed the bed on their honeymoon.

I'd met Friend in the isolation barracks after admitting my homosexuality. We had struck up a friendship after discovering that we were both from Minnesota. That, and the strange circumstances we were in, sparked an embarrassed and painful admission from Friend that he was being discharged because he wet the bed. In turn, partly to make him feel better about just wetting the bed, and because I desperately wanted to talk to someone about my problem, I told him I was a homosexual.

The stoic, Swedish expression on his face never changed, the last attentive look just froze into place. He never expected anything as horrible as my revelation, certainly not from another Minnesota boy who looked like most people he knew back home. He was so overwhelmed with his own disgrace that it had never occurred to him that there were worse crimes than wetting the bed.

He avoided me after that, and he soon disappeared from the barracks. Poor guy, a nice farm kid like that, thrown in with "monsters" like me because he wet the bed. I could have used a friend. There were only about a dozen of us in that barracks, all of us waiting for less-than-honorable discharges.

The navy made no demands on us there. We were on our own. We were beyond hope. No one checked to see if our bunks were made or if we were in proper undress blues. The smoking lamp was always lit. We got up when we wanted to. We wandered over to the mess hall at the same times as we always had, just out of habit. We had all the privileges of condemned men.

We usually shaved because that, too, had become a habit, because it was something to do to pass the time. We showered and we shaved and we washed our shorts, all except the kid from Arkansas. He was filthy. I had never seen anyone that dirty in my life. And that ugly. He had a flat, blank face, thick lips, dull, crafty eyes, and a flat, fleshy nose peppered with blackheads. His teeth were moldy, grayish-green around the gums.

His once white, navy-issue boxer shorts had long ago turned a desolate gray with urine blotches in front and brown streaks that could be seen through the droopy rear.

Still, he was the friendliest guy in the place, more talkative than the rest of us. He had been bragging, in fact, that he could suck his own cock. The kid was nuts. Who could suck his own cock? We pooh-poohed the whole story with bored superiority. Suck your own cock? Well, he looked weird enough to try it. Maybe he was double-jointed.

Well, Arkansas persisted, did we want to see it?

He knew that we didn't believe him, so he made it sound like a challenge. Did we want to see it?

"Yeah," one guy finally said, tired of the question, "let's see you do it."

We stood around his bottom bunk in a ragged semicircle, seven or eight of us, embarrassed to be part of such an exhibition, even as the audience, but so bored that we were grateful for the diversion.

He lay back and unbuttoned his flap, then took out a long, thin, grungy-looking cock, a gray cock the color of oatmeal, as gray as his shorts. He stroked it a few times, revealing a white, cheeselike substance under the dull purple head when he pulled back the foreskin. Putting his hands under his hips and raising his ass, he doubled himself up so that his cock dangled half-hard over his chest. Then, in one practiced motion, he arched his neck, brought his head up, his mouth gaping wide open like a baby bird waiting to be fed, pulled his ass in closer, and took the head of his cock in his mouth. Watching us covertly out of the corners of his eyes, he gloated at his success. Then, like a spring suddenly uncoiled, he flopped back down on his bunk and stuffed his cock back into his pants, all the while grinning ear to ear with great, proud, open-mouthed triumph. We stared back at him, and without a word, we wandered off.

I thought that once he got it in his mouth, he'd finish the job, but it was just a trick that he could perform. There was nothing sexual about it at all. It was as mechanical as those old cast-iron banks that were designed to pop coins into an opening. We drifted away, silent, a little disgusted at the spectacle, still bored. What the kid really needed to do was take a shower. That would have been the best trick of all.

We went back to reading our magazines, smoking, waiting for chow time, waiting for the ax to fall. We waited in silence. We rarely spoke to one another. We avoided eye contact.

In that whole gloomy barracks with its bare windows and gray walls, stacked with upper and lower bunks, we chose bunks at a distance from one another, prisoners a little suspicious of our cell mates, each desperately hoarding his own guilt. We avoided showering together in the big open shower room, but nature sometimes forced us to shit together, not side by side, of course, but exposed to one another on that long, open row of white toilets in the head.

We ate, slept, smoked, and shit together but we rarely spoke. We never laughed. When we did speak, it was usually in grunts or monosyllables or to ask the most basic questions.

"Got a cigarette?"

"What time is it?"

"Anybody got a stamp?"

The newcomers always asked, "Where do we eat?"

Those were the longest conversations that we had.

There was hardly a sound except for an occasional cough,

the morning farting, and the Night Crier. I hated that guy. He cried every night, into his pillow, muffled, harsh little moans and sobs. Every night he cried himself to sleep. Sometimes I'd wake up in the middle of the night and he was still crying. It was a sound as grating and as frightening as rats gnawing their way into our tomb.

We all heard it but no one said anything about it. I suspected the Night Crier was the guy who wanted me to go back to Georgia with him. He had latched onto me after Friend left, shuffling up beside me one morning as I was reading a Mutt and Jeff comic book.

I didn't like him. He must have been thirty years old, and his hands fluttered when he talked, never quite escaping his arm. His eyes were red from weeping and he kept blowing his nose. When he stood behind me and said, "Good morning," it sounded like he had a mouth full of cotton.

I didn't just dislike the Night Crier. I was afraid of him, frightened to see a man break down like that, someone I suspected was in the same boat I was. No, I told myself, he isn't like me. I had confessed my homosexuality. I had even gotten sick about it. But I had never cried about it.

I consoled myself with the fact that even if I was queer, even though I must have had some kind of breakdown, even if I had done something so stupid it had ruined my life, at least I had not cried about it.

The Night Crier sat down on the other side of my bench and told me that he had worked for a newspaper in Atlanta and he was a friend of Margaret Mitchell who had written *Gone with the Wind*.

"Have you read it?"

"No, but I saw the movie."

The Night Crier wanted me to come to Georgia with him to meet his family. He'd introduce me to Margaret Mitchell. He seemed desperate to take someone along with him so that whatever was waiting for him at home, he would not have to face it alone.

No, thanks, I told him, I have to go home. I didn't know what to tell my parents when I got there, but I had to go home. I had been through the interrogations, the threats, the cross-examinations. I'd been fondled by the navy and comforted by the Red Cross.

We alternated between days of boredom in the barracks and hours of intense interrogations in a building across the yard. One navy officer asked me why I had lied to get into the navy if I was homosexual. I hadn't lied, I told him. Someone had asked me if I liked girls and I'd said yes. I do like girls. One of the officers thought I was making the whole thing up, that I wasn't homosexual at all. Some of them thought I had lied to get in and some of them thought I was lying to get out. They threatened me with a court-martial. They called me back for more questioning.

"Have you eved had homosexual relations with anyone?"

"Yes," I replied, "when I was growing up."

"With whom?"

I never hesitated with the answer. I could prove I wasn't lying. I named Orville and Jim from the Garfield school, but this was a joke on the navy because Orville had been classified 4-F and wasn't even in the service and Jim, although now in the army, had become what my dad called "cunt crazy" and certainly wasn't fooling around with boys anymore. They couldn't do anything to either of them.

"Have you ever had relations in the service?"

"Yes, once," I admitted, "with an ensign in Chicago."

I realized my mistake as soon as I mentioned the ensign. That admission electrified the room. I hadn't just had sex with a man, I'd had intercourse with an officer. Now, more than mine, they wanted the head of my ensign from Chicago.

In the cold, gray light of that morning in Chicago, waking up naked in a warm bed, smelling of the night's sweat and whiskey, the heavy sweet-sour odor of come still on our breath, the ensign realized the terrible mistake he had made, the awful risk he had taken. He'd not only had a homosexual encounter, but had engaged in sex with an enlisted man. Although I sensed his discomfort, he kept his concerns to himself. He never flinched, never made excuses. He didn't hurry off. We cleaned up and went out to find a restaurant.

It had been a wonderful night. As soon as we got in the room, we stripped off our uniforms and fell naked onto each other, clumsy and eager, both of us shooting off too quickly. Relaxing between bouts, we smoked, felt content, and anticipated an entire night like that, lying side by side, silent, dreamlike.

Once, lying still after our cigarettes, we made a crude tent with our erections, his side poking up much higher than mine. I dove under the sheet and he caught me by my ass, swung me around, pulled me into him, and we locked again together in a comfortable 69, slow and easy and deep. We finally fell asleep, exhausted, him curled up behind me spoon fashion, his breath warm and soothing on my neck. I passed into a dark, pleasant world until morning finally found me.

God, we were hungry when we woke. We ate a big breakfast of ham and eggs, fried potatoes, toast with strawberry jam, and coffee. We didn't say much, but we enjoyed the food. Afterward, in broad daylight and with him cold sober, looking handsome in his gold-trimmed uniform and me in my seaman's blues, he walked me over to my train to Great Lakes. He shook hands with me and wished me well.

There was something so fine about him, drunk or sober, that I felt instinctively protective of whatever that quality was. I would've gone to prison before I would give up the name of a man like that.

"Yes," I told my interrogators, "I slept with an ensign in Chicago."

"What is the ensign's name?"

"I don't know his name."

"What ship is he on?"

"He never told me."

"You never saw any identification? Dog tags? Any name stenciled on his clothing?"

"Not that I noticed."

"What ship is he on?"

"Where is he stationed?"

"I was drunk," I replied. "I don't remember."

They threatened me with a court-martial, a jail sentence, unless I told them the name. They sent me back to the barracks to think that over. The next day they called me back again.

"What is the name of the ensign?"

"What ship is he on?"

"Where is he stationed?"

They turned me over to a psychiatrist, a sly, oily lieutenant who reminded me of Swivel Hips back home. This was a Swivel Hips with authority, in regal navy drag, aglow with gold and prestige, reeking of cologne, with a voice as greasy and bland as lard. He was a large, soft, smarmy, unctuous bastard who grasped my hands in his, fondled them and murmured, "These hands haven't seen hard work. They're so smooth and soft." What a dumb thing to say. I resented the remark, the fondling. I jerked my hands away and he abruptly dismissed me, turning his back disdainfully as I left the room.

The navy turned crafty on me. If I was a homosexual, then a woman might be the best bet to gain my confidence. I was taken into a WAVE's office, another lieutenant. She was wiry, mannish, rough, with a metallic twang to her voice, with none of the polish of the male officers. She was as stiff and basic as a hairpin.

She got confidential with me, buddy-buddy. She had me sit down. She perched on the desk beside my chair. She lit a cigarette and she offered me one. I declined. She smiled ruefully at the pickle I was in. She got up, swaggered around the room on skinny bow legs, her skirt taut at the knees. She circled me.

"That bastard," she began, sounding sympathetic, "taking advantage of a kid like you."

She glanced obliquely at me, blew cigarette smoke up into the air out of her curled lower lip, paused by my chair, put one hand on my shoulder like a comrade, and shook her head mournfully.

"Taking advantage of a kid like you," she repeated.

I remained silent.

She paced the room, circling my chair again, her thin legs bowed like a wishbone and as bare of meat. Suddenly, she stopped, pounded her fist into the palm of her hand and cried passionately, "I'd like to get my hands on that bastard!"

She cast a sympathetic look at me and paused dramatically. I sat there, fully attentive, dazzled by her performance, but I said nothing.

Then, as if the idea had just struck her, she demanded, "What ship is he on?"

"He never said."

"What is the name of the hotel you went to?"

A new question. A good one.

"I don't remember. A cheap hotel."

She rolled her eyes at the answer and grunted disdainfully. "The bastard. Not even taking you to a nice hotel."

She finally dismissed me, shaking her head at the pickle I was in, vowing to help me any way she could.

"You just ask for me," she offered.

In the midst of the interrogations, I was taken to the hospital. The chest pains I'd been having for several days were worse. It was painful and difficult to breathe. Every time I took a breath, something raw seemed to rub against another raw spot in my chest. The doctor diagnosed my condition as pleurisy and kept me in the hospital a couple of days. When I was returned to the isolation barracks, I wondered if the pleurisy had been part of my problem.

I was thinking clearer now, painfully clearer. That brief stay in the hospital had snapped me out of the daze I was in, the paralyzing depression. I came back to the barracks horrified at what I had done. I'd just felt numb before, like a zombie. Now I was clearheaded and overwhelmed at the mess I was in.

God, was it too late to fix it? I needed help.

Someone must be able to help me. There was only one person I could think of. The Red Cross officer. He had been the only one who was really concerned about me. He listened when I tried to explain things. He sympathized with me. He never asked about the ensign.

We'd sit in his office, after he'd sent for me, and he'd send out for coffee and we'd talk, like friends, about my hometown, my rotten summer in Greenwich Village, my friends, my plans to be a writer. We even talked about my dreams.

He was the closest thing I had to a friend. I hated to ask him for a favor, to impose on his kindness, but there was no place else to go. Maybe he could use his influence to get me something besides a bad discharge. Maybe, if it wasn't too late, they might let me go to jail for a while if I could stay in the navy.

I hiked over to his office and found the tough little guy who seemed to be his aide, the "Dead-End Kid," I called him because he reminded me of those New York slum kids in the movies.

"No, the director isn't in," he said. "He's gone to Chicago."

I wasn't sure what to do. It hadn't occurred to me that the director wouldn't be in his office.

"Whaddaya wanna see him about?"

It wasn't any of his business, but I had come over to talk to someone, so I said I thought the director might be able to help me with something.

The kid sneered at me.

"You think he's gonna help ya?"

"I'm gonna ask."

"Boy, youse small-town guys make me laugh. Youse guys trust everybody."

I stared at him. How did he know I was from a small town? I didn't like him at all. I turned to go when he suddenly said: "He don't care nuttin' about you."

"What do you mean?"

The kid looked at me for a few seconds, like he felt sorry for me. "Come on," he said indulgently. "I wanna show ya somethin."

He started toward the director's office.

"What are you going to do?"

"You know all dose bull sessions he had wid ya? How cozy he gets? He writes it all up. He's writing a book about guys like us."

I was so surprised to hear this that I overlooked the "guys like us" remark.

"I'll show ya," he offered.

He opened the door to the office and waved me inside like he owned the place. I hung back.

"We could get in trouble going in there."

He snorted.

"Whadda they gonna do—shoot us?"

He crossed over to a file cabinet and I trailed after him. He opened a bottom drawer, flipped through some papers and pulled out a file. It had my name on it and a title, "The Homo-sexual Speaks."

I opened it up and read a description of myself, a summary of my problems in the navy, and details of every conversation I had ever had with him. He must have written it all down as soon as I left his office. He'd even found out about the ensign.

I handed the file back to the Dead-End Kid and he put it back. We stood there awkwardly. The kid was right. All this time the Red Cross director was pretending to be my friend so he could get information from me.

The kid was looking at me like he expected something.

"Thanks," I finally said.

Was that it? What did he expect? I was tired. I was sorry

I had come. I just wanted to get back to the barracks, climb up on my bunk, and lie down for a while.

We went out and he closed the office door.

"Thanks again," I said, shaking his hand.

"Yeah," he replied, looking at me in a curious way, as if from a distance, as though I had stepped out of focus, out of reach.

When I got back to the barracks, a new guy was checking in. He was Mexican or Spanish, a dark, good-looking guy, little, but perfectly proportioned, well built and wearing a small gold cross on a short chain around his neck.

He asked if anyone had the upper bunk under the ceiling light in the center of the room near the smoking lamp. When told that it was vacant, he settled in to read. He said no more. He didn't even ask where to eat.

We all watched him surreptitiously. I don't think any of us had ever seen anyone that fine before. It wasn't just that he was good-looking. He was beautiful. Not handsome—beautiful. Handsome was too wooden, too shallow a description for some-one like that. He had a natural courtesy, a pride, a solemn re-serve, an odd sense of soul that set him apart from the rest of us. We were in awe of him.

He kept to a routine that shamed the rest of us. He shit, shaved, and showered, in that order, each morning, and he maintained an illusion of privacy, of dignity even, while sitting on the open toilet, never looking embarrassed or glancing around awkwardly as most of us did.

After his shower, he dressed, made his bunk, cleaned up around the smoking lamp, swept the barracks, did push-ups and sit-ups before breakfast, ate alone, walked around the compound, came back, and read. Twice, he had gone in and mopped up the head. He wasn't afraid of hard work. He exer-cised again in the afternoon and before bedtime. Even when he read, there was something almost fierce in his concentration. Nothing distracted him. One morning I saw him awaken, sit up in his bunk, kneel, cross himself, and pray; it was a private action, performed naturally and earnestly.

He was as beautiful, remote, and smooth as an antique Greek statue. Everything about him was beautiful, from the fine, almost invisible down on the small of his back that disappeared V-shaped into the deep, hidden recess of his ass, to the finely chiseled head and the perfect white teeth. He smelled like honey. His name was Emmanuel.

A couple of us borrowed things from him just to be able to speak to him. He would courteously hand over a magazine or a couple of stamps, but he, in turn, never borrowed anything, never asked anything of us.

One morning after he had been with us about three days, I came out of the head and was lighting up a Camel, standing near the smoking table, when I noticed everyone at the table staring up at his bunk. I looked up to see what it was.

He was sitting on the edge of his bunk, in his immaculate white boxer shorts, his legs dangling over the side, his fly wide open, his fist full of hard, thick cock. The head was red and angry like he was ready to come, and he was smiling at someone in the room, a radiant smile, open, joyous, inviting. His eyes looked squarely ahead, and there was a bright glow, almost a halo, around his head. With his left hand, he beckoned his heart's desire over to him in short, deft motions.

I couldn't take my eyes off him, so I never knew who had turned him on; it was someone in back of me. We stood there and gaped at the spectacle, thrilled, horrified, almost hypnotized, until suddenly, a cloud seemed to pass over his face. The smile vanished, and he looked down at his own erection.

He slipped down off his bunk, his face pale but composed. Not looking at any of us, his cock back in his shorts, his shaving kit in one hand, he walked into the toilet.

I went outside to walk around. I didn't want to face the guy after that. So that's what it was all about. He had tried so hard to keep himself occupied, to stay busy, to avoid contact with anyone and so lessen the danger, but one of us had unknowingly broken through his defense. I felt miserable, sick to my stomach, as if I had been the one publicly exposed like that, tricked by some hidden part of my mind.

When I came back into the barracks, they were mopping his blood up from the toilet. He had slashed his wrists. He was gone. Dead or alive, they had hauled him away.

Now it was my turn. My number had come up. My captain's mast. Captain Bond stood there, high above me, in that huge cold auditorium. Leaning forward from his podium, resplendent in gold braid and cold authority, a grand martinet, he thundered the navy's verdict in rich, theatrical tones. I was being discharged: UNDESIRABLE.

The word echoed through the whole building, bounced off the walls, vibrated in my ears, and knocked the breath out of me. I was dismissed, and as I forced myself to move and executed a stiff right face, turning toward a panel of officer witnesses standing nearby, I glanced into the face of an ensign. I saw there a look of horror and compassion.

Odd, how in just a second you can find so much exposed in another man's face: horror, compassion, and something else, something like recognition.

13

Dinner at the Ryan

*I*T WAS A SMALL CELEBRATION, just Meg and me. We were in the Ryan Hotel dining room, eating lobster, baked potatoes with sour cream and butter, fresh rolls, and crisp, colorful vegetables from an elaborate cut-glass relish tray, artfully arranged with pickled mushrooms, pimiento-stuffed olives, baby sweet pickles, celery, and slender reeds of carrots. We were stuffing ourselves on foods that we seldom had, giggling and laughing at our extravagance. This was no sour bean soup.

I had thought of ordering wine, but the only wines I knew by name were "Dago Red" and muscatel and I was sure they wouldn't go with lobster. Instead, we just kept drinking whiskey.

The waiters, in white coats and dark trousers, some of them retired dining car waiters from the railroad, bustled about, solemn and assured, bringing us baskets of rolls, chilled butter patties, ice for our water, and clean ashtrays to replace those we had barely soiled.

I had often passed the hotel's dining room on my way to the bar or the coffee shop and looked in on all that overstuffed luxury, but I had never had dinner there, had never set foot in the place.

I had admired from a distance the thick, pure whiteness of the table coverings, layers of freshly ironed white linen, the glow of the candelabra, the soft, amber lighting, the thick, dark draperies, that rich velvet that blanketed the street noise. I had envied the murmured contentment of the diners as they enjoyed the measured and almost regal attention from those formal caretakers in their starched white jackets.

It was my party. I was the host. I had just been fired from my shipping clerk job and to show that I didn't give a damn, I had invited Meg out to dinner.

I hadn't been told why I was fired, I had just been called in that morning and cashed out after a year on the job, a year in which I had never been late and had never missed a day's work. Meg said the only thing that she heard was the manager telling a couple of people he was concerned that I would be a "bad influence" on the people with whom I worked. Meg thought that was ridiculous, and after one or two more whiskeys, we decided it was hilarious. Me dangerous? Who was I? Al Capone? I ordered more whiskey.

Meg had stuck with me despite the disgrace of my departure. To get my check, I had to pass through a roomful of people whom I had known for a year, had coffee with, had spoken to each morning and afternoon, joked with, and they all let me pass without comment, without recognition, without even looking up. It was as if I were invisible, no longer among the living. It was a chilling isolation.

I wondered if someone had seen me going into Kirmser's, or if they had finally checked out my military discharge, or if someone had pulled that same dirty trick on me that they had pulled on Dale, that anonymous phone call. I never knew.

Dale had found out. It hadn't been Flaherty who had gotten Dale fired, as we had always suspected. It was Dale's brother, the big shot with the state. His own brother had gotten him fired. Dale found out after his mother died and he and his brother got into an argument over an old quilt their grandmother had brought from Sweden. During the argument, his brother called Dale a "goddamn homo."

Stunned not only by the realization that his brother knew about him, but that his brother despised him for it, Dale said nothing until an awful thought occurred to him and he asked, "Were you the one who got me fired?"

His brother never answered that question, but replied instead, "I'm the one who got you your job," as if that favor, motivated by guilt, had balanced the books.

Now it had happened to me. In one fell swoop, I was an outcast, out of a job. Everything and everyone had changed. Except Meg. As I was leaving, she came forward, and in front of the whole silent room, a silence so heavy and watchful that I could feel it, could drown in it, in a clear, even voice, Meg invited me to meet her after work at Matt Weber's.

Impulsively, I said, "No, make it the Ryan. Let's go first class." I'd show them that being fired from that lousy job was no disgrace. It was cause for celebration.

Then I was safely out the door, leaving Meg to work alone in that ugly silence, bearing the stigma of being an admitted friend of mine.

When we left the Ryan after dinner, a little numb from the booze, I walked Meg to the corner bus stop. Just as her bus appeared, she turned to me and said, "Rick, whatever you're looking for, I hope you find it."

No laughter. No joke. But a blessing. After the shock of being fired, the guilt, the fear, and the humiliation, after all the booze we'd drunk in a raucous attempt to be lighthearted, worrying about what I could tell my parents, Meg left me with a benediction. It touched me as nothing ugly ever could, bringing tears to my eyes. I turned away from the bus so Meg wouldn't think I was crying.

My dinner with Meg had truly been my farewell party, because that afternoon I had decided that I was getting out of St. Paul, going back to New York. I didn't know what else to do. I was afraid that I would get a bad job recommendation from the company. I might never be able to get another job in St. Paul. Going to New York would be a reason I could give to my folks for "quitting" my job.

I was going to New York, going on the stage, going to be an actor. I'd heard that there were a lot of queer people in the theater and the movies. I'd heard the gossip in Kirmser's about people like Tyrone Power and Tallulah Bankhead. It was a door that was open. I didn't need references. You auditioned for a part and if they liked you, you got the job. Nobody asked to see your references. Nobody asked if you were a veteran.

If I could face down all those surly assholes at St. Michael's school, reciting a silly poem perfectly well, I could handle anything New York had to offer.

Going to New York meant the end of my romance with Lucky, and although I regretted that loss, I felt an unexpected sense of relief, a sense of lightness. No more obligations. No more Lucky. I was on my own.

Getting fired had scared the shit out of me. Now I not only had an undesirable discharge, but my employment history would show I had been fired from a job. I had a whole year and a half to lie about. I tried to bluff my way through it, announcing in Kirmser's my plans to go to New York, to go on the stage, to be an actor. I gave a cocky little performance that even I realized made me sound as mouthy and obnoxious as Flaherty.

The truth was much simpler. If anything scandalous happened to me, if I was unable to get work, if I was arrested for indecent conduct or robbery or for any crime at all, I wanted that disgrace to be in a city so big that no one would know me. I could disappear in New York. I was willing to die if I could die anonymously.

On my last night in Kirmser's before taking the bus to New York, Joe took me aside to talk to me. Lucky was barely speaking to me and was being consoled by Dale. I'd been talking to Tony at her spot at the bar when Joe called me over.

"Rick, you got a minute?"

Rick? He'd called me by name and I realized it was only the second time in all the time I knew him, after all the afternoons we'd spent together, that he used my name. The only other time was that day in Walgreen's when he'd introduced me to his partner. It was as if a name was a potential indictment, an infringement on a person's privacy, not to be used carelessly, to be spoken only in emergencies or on formal occasions.

I was thinking of this, how odd it was, when another thought occurred to me. My God, maybe Joe was finally going to buy me a doughnut! But, no, it was nothing as frivolous or extravagant or uncharacteristic as that. He wanted to talk to me about the psychology of dress.

"The psychology of dress?" I laughed. "What books have you been reading?"

But Joe had never been more serious.

"Wear the kind of clothes that attract the kind of people you're looking for," he said, pointing out that Pulanski dressed to attract people with money and Flaherty wore tight sweaters to show off his muscles to attract body worshipers. Joe himself dressed in pea coat and cap to attract blue-collar workers "and whatever sailors—God bless 'em—might come by." Joe smiled when he said this, but then he turned serious again.

"Most important," Joe said, and I think he was beginning to understand me better than I understood myself, "when you're cruising, be neat, wear old clothes, and never wear jewelry."

Good old Joe. I never forgot this advice. Everyone knew I was going to New York, but only Joe knew the route I was taking.

Thirty-six years after being kicked out of the navy, I petitioned for a review of my discharge. On May 26, 1981, I was granted an honorable discharge from the navy.

RICARDO J. BROWN was born in Stillwater, Minnesota, in 1926. He worked in the newspaper business most of his life and was a former reporter and editor for the Associated Press, the *Alabama Journal,* and the *Fairbanks Daily News-Miner,* and was Minneapolis bureau chief for Fairchild Publications. He lived in Minneapolis at the time of his death in 1998.

WILLIAM REICHARD has written a collection of poetry, *An Alchemy in the Bones,* and a novella, *Harmony.* His work has been published in numerous anthologies and journals, including *The Georgia Review* and *The Ontario Review.* He lives in St. Paul.

ALLAN H. SPEAR was, until his retirement in 2000, the longest-serving gay male legislator in the nation, having been a member of the Minnesota senate since 1972. He is associate professor emeritus of history at the University of Minnesota and the author of *Black Chicago: The Making of a Negro Ghetto.* He lives in Minneapolis.